Contents

Illustrations

Illustrations appear between pages 120 and 121

Pictures 1, 3, 8, 9 and 11 are the author's photographs.
Picture 5 courtesy of Paolo Chirco.

1

Two Deaths

The driver of the midnight train from Palermo stopped the locomotive when he felt a bump on the line. He climbed down and saw the rail was twisted and broken, but luckily the train hadn't jumped the tracks. It was 1978 and nobody had mobile phones. So he stopped at the next station, Cinisi, where he told the stationmaster what had happened. Oddly, the police were only contacted two hours later.

When they searched the area they quickly saw that about two feet of the track had been destroyed in what looked like an explosion. But the blast hadn't just damaged a stretch of railway line. As the police report written later that morning stated:

> A body had been blown to pieces and fragments were spread over a radius of 300 metres. They are described as follows: a piece of the cerebral lobe, bones from the vault of the skull and segments of scalp were all found at a short distance . . . A piece of bone identified as a segment of the spine . . . there are loose pieces of tissue everywhere whose original bodily position cannot be identified . . . a limb, presumably the right thigh-bone . . . partly covered

with the remains of blue trousers, and a sock of the same colour on the foot . . .

About 100 metres from this bone the remains of the left thigh-bone were discovered . . . spread all around the area, particularly close to the railway line, were fragments of clothing made up of two patterns: a green, brown and grey check; blue material probably belonging to the trousers; blue wool probably belonging to a jumper . . . Furthermore, on the road-bed adjacent to the line two Dr. Scholl clogs were found . . .

Four days later, people were still scraping bits of flesh off surrounding bushes and trees.

While the police were writing their report, another murder took place in Rome. Three men took their hostage down into a garage and shot him repeatedly. They then drove the body to the city centre and left the car, phoning the press with the news. This murder was carried out by the Red Brigades, a left-wing terrorist organisation. The man they had killed was Aldo Moro, whom they had kidnapped 55 days earlier. Moro had been elected as Italy's Christian Democrat prime minister five times, and was arguably the most powerful politician in the country – this is why the Red Brigades kidnapped him. They hoped to gain credibility by negotiating the release of some of their members held in jail in exchange for Moro, or alternatively to obtain large amounts of money through payment of a ransom. When it became clear the government wouldn't negotiate, they killed him. So after a month and a half of anguish, with the Pope even offering to substitute himself as hostage, the huge public crisis came to a tragic end.

Naturally there was wall-to-wall television coverage of Moro's death, so the other death earlier that day in Cinisi didn't make it onto television news, and newspapers only commented on it briefly the next day. After all, this was a sleepy town whose only notable feature was the fact that Palermo airport had been built within its boundaries. What apparently connected the two deaths was terrorism; the police quickly said the dead man in Sicily was probably a left-wing terrorist who had been blown up by his own bomb. But what really connected them, or rather what connected Aldo Moro and national politics to the body blown to pieces in a small Sicilian town was the Mafia.

2

The Killing Fields

When three American tanks drove into the central Sicilian town of Villalba on 20 July 1943, the soldiers immediately asked local people to call Don Calogero Vizzini for them. Eight days later US Lieutenant Beehr from the Allies' civil affairs office presided over a ceremony at the local police station, in which Vizzini became mayor of his home town.

The Allied invasion of Sicily in the summer of 1943 overthrew a dictatorship that had lasted twenty years. Their problem was that opposition to Mussolini and fascism was dominated by Socialists and Communists, whose demands hardly coincided with American plans for postwar Italy. Rather than working with these mass democratic organisations, the Allies turned to a different kind of power structure.

Superficially, Vizzini seemed a very respectable middle-aged man, two of his brothers were priests and one of his uncles was a bishop. But a quick look at Vizzini's criminal record during the fascist period illustrated what kind of man he really was: tried for four different murders he had been acquitted each time, although he was convicted of Mafia membership and spent five years in jail. He had also been charged, but not brought to trial, for 39 murders, six attempted murders, 36 robberies, 37 thefts and 63 extortions. Documents written by US agents at the time clearly show that officials knew who the Mafia leaders were – indeed Vizzini was probably the leader of the Mafia at the time – they therefore had no objection to giving political power to top *Mafiosi*.

A similar event occurred in the town of Mussomeli, just a few miles away. A new councillor, Giuseppe Genco Russo, had been acquitted of five murders in 1928, four in 1929 and three in 1930, together with three attempted murders; in 1931 he escaped conviction for being a member of a criminal organisation, and in 1932 once again was acquitted of three murders. However, he was convicted of conspiracy to commit a crime in 1932 and served three years of a six-year sentence.

These appointments were being supervised by Colonel Charles Poletti, the senior allied adminstrator of Occupied Italy. An American businessman from an Italian background, he had been deputy governor of New York State before the war and was also a Freemason. Naturally, Poletti appointed specialised staff, such as his interpreter Vito Genovese, to help him. Apart from being fluent in two languages Genovese had a long criminal record, given the fact he was one of the main bosses of the US Mafia – indeed he had fled New York in 1936 to escape several charges of murder.

Whereas for the Allies reliance on the Mafia meant keeping Communists and Socialists at bay, for the Mafia it meant making large amounts of money. The economy of an area in which a war has just been fought is always in need of emergency supplies, and a huge quantity of Allied goods went missing. Some researchers have estimated that up to 60 per cent of goods unloaded in Naples during this period ended up on the black market.

So, for many Sicilians, the removal of Mussolini also meant the resurgence of the Mafia, which had found new fertile ground given both the poverty and difficulties people faced during and immediately after the war, and the tolerant attitude of the Allies. Although the reality of the Allies' formal support for democracy was far murkier than it seemed, it nevertheless gave many poor Sicilians the space they needed to resume the battle for social justice that fascism had repressed twenty years earlier.

The Mafia and Class War

With the end of Mussolini's repressive regime and the hardships of wartime, the deep frustration and impatience many people felt for radical change sometimes took on extreme forms, and produced equally uncompromising responses. In October 1944, when council workers went on strike in Palermo against abuses in the rationing system, troops began firing and throwing hand grenades into the crowd, killing 30 people and wounding 150. Between December 1944 and January 1945 there were a whole series of revolts in Sicilian towns, generally lasting only a day or two. One of the more violent, which raged for a week, took place in the far south-east, in the town of Ragusa, and broke out when call-up papers arrived. Young people didn't want to join the army – some had already fought in Mussolini's fascist army. The entire town rose up in armed rebellion, using their own weapons and what the German army had left behind. The fighting went on for several days and at least 37 were killed and 86 wounded.

By now the war was far away, the remnants of Mussolini's regime and Nazi invaders were being fought in the north of Italy, and would finally be defeated in April 1945. The big issue throughout Sicily was now land reform. Half of all of Sicily's agricultural land was owned by just 1 per cent of the population, huge swathes of land had often been left uncultivated – in the midst of masses of hungry and unemployed peasants. The new democratic government in Rome, made up of all the anti-fascist parties but closely monitored by the Allies, faced a choice: either try and repress this movement even further, or head it off by giving it limited powers and accepting some of its demands, while all the time promising 'jam tomorrow' as regards the big political and economic issues.

The government's most important concession came on the central issue of land reform, when it passed a law that broke up the *latifondo*, the large private estates. Peasants could either work the land and for the first time keep much of the produce for themselves, or the land itself would be redistributed to local cooperatives – a key development as it encouraged peasants no longer just to think of their own family but in collective or class terms. Furthermore, most of these cooperatives were controlled by the Communist and Socialist parties. In many areas of the Sicilian countryside, for the first time in many decades, local people looked forward to a brighter future.

All of this was deeply worrying for the local establishment, as such reforms damaged their long-established interests. Feudalism – a system under which large landowners were legally entitled to have their own private armies and dispense 'justice' on their own terms – had officially been abolished in Sicily barely a hundred years before. The origins of the Mafia can be traced to the end of feudalism, with the first recorded mention of the word occurring in the 1860s. The first *Mafiosi* evolved from the people who enforced the landowners' contract, or wishes, over these large tracts of land where the owner himself rarely – if ever – set foot. In an island where the new national state of Italy had very little presence, these first *Mafiosi* were armed rent collectors. But when peasants became radical and organised, and began making demands, in effect these early *Mafiosi* acted as the military wing of the owners of these big landed estates of the interior.

The proposed redistribution of land meant that large landowners were facing a huge loss in wealth and power. In reality, just one hectare in ten was actually handed over to peasants, given that local magistrates made the final decision and often rejected peasant requests on technicalities. Alternatively, the police intervened to discourage peasants and trade unionists deliberately. In one notorious incident in San Giuseppe Jato a police commander forbade the text of the land reform law from being displayed in trade union offices, claiming it would lead to disorder.

Nevertheless, the peasants' newfound organisation and confidence were so high that they often simply marched onto land and occupied it anyway, regardless of whether it was fully legal or not. With trumpets blaring, hundreds and sometimes thousands formed up into a procession with their horses and tools to take the land. Often children were at the front of the march, and the local church had an organised presence too; so as well as the red flags of Communists and Socialists sometimes there were white flags with crosses. Behind the children came the women, then the town band, then peasants on horses or mules, or on foot. Behind them the artisans (cobblers, basket-weavers, barbers) and students. Schools were often shut down for the day of the occupation: whole towns would turn out, in what became a festival with two high points – crossing the boundary into the estate, and planting the crops that would be harvested in the months to come.

Meanwhile, the big landowners and their Mafia henchmen were not the kind of people to take this sort of thing lying down. In Sicily it was one thing to pass a law and quite another to apply it. As one *Mafioso* once told a peasant: 'The law! You've stuffed your heads full of this law. Round here, we're the law, we've always been the law.' The first victim of the Mafia's campaign to intimidate left-wing peasants – and stop them legally occupying large tracts of land – was Andrea Raia, who was murdered near Palermo in August 1944. The following month the leader of Sicilian Communists, Girolamo Li Causi, went to give a speech in Villalba, the hometown of the Mafia's leader, Don Calogero Vizzini. First Vizzini's brother, the parish priest, tried to drown out Li Causi by ringing the church bells. Li Causi continued, and when he started talking about the land and the links between *Mafiosi* and big landowners Vizzini cried out: 'It's not true.' This was the signal for a coordinated attack on the meeting: Vizzini's nephew and town mayor threw a hand grenade, while other *Mafiosi* started shooting. Fourteen Communists and Socialists were wounded, including Li Causi. The next significant murder followed in June 1945, the victim was a trade unionist; another was gunned down in September, a man who had been fighting to gain control over one of the Mafia's prime assets – freshwater wells, a vital resource in such a dry climate.

In December the secretary of a local Communist Party branch was murdered. Given that nearly all of these crimes went unpunished, either due to the authorities colluding with the Mafia or eyewitnesses not wanting to testify, the Mafia naturally grew in confidence and raised its sights the following year. So in May 1946 it was the turn of the Socialist mayor of Favara, who had been elected two months earlier with a huge majority. The following month the Socialist mayor of another nearby town, Naro, was also killed by a shotgun blast as he rode through the countryside.

Aware that the murder of individuals and mayors had not been enough, the Mafia now moved on to attack whole groups; after all, land occupations were carried out by large numbers of peasants. So in September, when a group of peasants were holding an evening meeting to discuss how to organise the occupation of Prince San Vincenzo's estate, local *Mafiosi* who had traditionally guarded the prince's estate threw a bomb into the room, killing two men and wounding 13.

In April 1947, four days before the crucial vote for the new Sicilian regional parliament, at Piana degli Albanesi, the house of a local Communist councillor was attacked with two hand grenades. In the town at the other end of the Portella della Ginestra pass, San Giuseppe Jato, 'Death to Communists' was painted on the front doors of many people taking part in the election campaign.

Portella della Ginestra

Throughout Sicily the traditional ruling class was grappling with what democracy meant after twenty years of fascism. On 25 February and 30 March 1947 waves and waves of peasants descended on the Sicilian capital, demanding land reform. Palermo had never before seen such numbers of peasants, who arrived by train, bus or even on horseback in their tens of thousands.

The key hurdle for all players was the first democratic election for the Sicilian regional parliament, due to be held on 20 April. After the onslaught they had carried out in the countryside, landowners, *Mafiosi*, magistrates and the police must have thought the peasants had stopped revolting. A new party called the Christian Democrats, supported by the Church, seemed sure to win. But the result sent shock waves around the entire country: the joint Socialist–Communist ticket won 29 seats, and the Christian Democrats just 19. In reality, because the Christian Democrats were a new party – having been formed just five years earlier – powerful forces such as the Vatican, the White House and Italian industrialists had still been wary about throwing their weight fully behind them.

Much of the local establishment were prepared to back a movement for the independence of Sicily, committed 'to end the exploitation of Sicily by the mainland'. It was financed by big landowners, who hoped that poor people would be attracted to it out of a sense of Sicilian nationalism, thus isolating them from the class-based appeal of socialism and communism. The leaders of this movement for autonomy held at least one meeting with Mafia leader Don Calogero Vizzini, which also included an Italian general. A report was written up by the US consul in Palermo, Alfred Nester, showing once again the US government's intimate knowledge of the Mafia. Nester's letter, classified 'secret' and sent to the secretary of state in Washington, began thus: 'I have the honor to report that on November 18, 1944 General Giuseppe Castellano, together with Mafia leaders including Calogero Vizzini conferred with Virgilio Nasi, head of the well-known Nasi family in Trapani and asked him to take over the leadership of a Mafia-backed movement for Sicilian autonomy.'

Over the next few years big landowners increasingly turned to Salvatore Giuliano's bandit gang. Giuliano's criminal career had begun with him going on the run in 1943 aged just 20, after he had murdered a policeman who caught him with a black-market consignment of wheat. In the lawless climate of those years, the notion of living up in the mountains as part of a gang of bandits was tempting to significant numbers of desperate peasants. Giuliano's gang quickly showed itself to be the most ruthless and successful, killing dozens of policemen during repeated attempts to capture him; it has been estimated his gang was responsible for an incredible 430 murders. He was an efficient killer, who ended up in a game far bigger than himself, manipulated by landowners and shady members of the police and secret services. As his deputy Gaspare Pisciotta said at a trial a few years later: 'We are a single body – bandits, police and Mafia – like the Father, the Son and the Holy Ghost.'

It was as part of this unstable series of alliances that Salvatore Giuliano's gang was lying in wait on May Day 1947 at Portella della Ginestra, a pass between two mountains. Up to 15,000 peasants from San Giuseppe Jato and Piana degli Albanesi had congregated in the fields around the pass to celebrate their election victory, but when the first speaker began his speech a series of sharp cracks suddenly rang out. A few people started applauding, thinking it was fireworks. But when the outer circle of horses and mules began to fall to the ground it became clear someone was shooting. The firing lasted for twenty long minutes. During this time, on a rocky flat plain, people desperately crawled around for whatever shelter they could find, and this was why many victims were hit in the side or the buttocks rather than in the chest, arms or legs.

It was a massacre. In total, 12 people were murdered and dozens were injured. Later, over a thousand empty bullet cases were recovered.

The following day the whole country was at a standstill because unions called a general strike. People understood that nobody organises mass murder on such a scale without being highly motivated and highly organised. But, despite the fact that the target was a highly political one, in parliament the minister of the interior said that it had nothing to do with politics – it was just local criminals.

The Vatican, through its newspaper *l'Osservatore Romano*, criticised the general strike. Indeed, soon after the massacre

Cardinal Ernesto Ruffini, archbishop of Palermo from 1946 to 1967, wrote to the Pope saying he 'certainly could not approve of violence' from any side, but that 'resistance and rebellion were inevitable in the face of the Communists and their bullying, lies and deceitful scheming, their anti-Italian and anti-Christian ideas'. The message coming from the two most powerful institutions, government and Church, was clear – the killing could continue.

Meanwhile, as far as national politics was concerned, the Cold War was gathering pace. Following the defeat of fascism, Italy had been ruled by an uneasy coalition government made up of Christian Democrats, Communists and Socialists, but it was an unelected government. The first democratic elections were scheduled for spring 1948, and the United States was anxious to ensure that Communists and Socialists did not win and bring Italy into the orbit of the Soviet Union.

During the month following the Portella della Ginestra massacre the national coalition government that had ruled the country since 1945 collapsed. The Christian Democrat leader Alcide De Gasperi came back from a visit to America, and soon afterwards announced that Communists and Socialists were to be removed from power, leaving the Christian Democrats as the main party of government, a position they would hold for nearly fifty years.

The leaders of the left went to ground. The Communist leader, Palmiro Togliatti, prevented a Communist MP from Sicily raising questions about the massacre in parliament. In Palermo, the Socialists and Communists thought it better to ignore the clear majority they had won in the Sicilian parliament, and allowed the Christian Democrats to form a minority administration.

Things were much more stark in the Sicilian countryside, as many peasants were not prepared to go back to the days of fascist oppression or domination by arrogant landowners and their Mafia enforcers. So the following month the killing began again in western Sicily, but this time it was coordinated on an even greater scale.

A Long Night of Terror

After having already suffered at Portella della Ginestra, the town of San Giuseppe Jato became a target again. Soon after dusk on the evening of 22 June a group of men opened fire on the local Communist Party branch, but luckily their three hand grenades failed to explode, and the 11 machine-gun bullets that penetrated the rooms inside only managed to wound one woman. At 9.30pm on the same evening the Communist Party branch at Borgetto, just five miles away from San Giuseppe Jato, was also attacked. Three men were posted as lookouts while two other men wearing police uniforms moved forward and fired 40 bullets from a machine gun at the office, which fortunately was empty. Oddly enough, they were firing just 20 metres away from the police station.

The most serious attack that evening took place virtually simultaneously, just a mile away, in the main street of Partinico. People were killed here because, unlike all the other Communist Party branches attacked that night, this one was still open. It was about 10pm, and the office was unlit as it was about to close. As the attackers turned the corner into the main street they came face to face with their enemies; so as not to have eyewitnesses they immediately shot to kill. The Communists scrambled inside the darkened room, but from the street outside machine-gun bursts ripped into the darkness, three grenades and two petrol bombs were thrown as well. As the attackers disappeared into the night it quickly transpired they had seriously wounded several people and murdered two.

Five miles to the east, it was the turn of the Socialist Party branch at Monreale. At 2am, petrol was poured over the doors, but those living on the first floor quickly woke up and put the flames out.

Two more attacks took place in towns very close to the coast. The first was at Carini, where at 10pm machine guns opened up on the Communist Party branch, but on this occasion the attackers first threw bottles of petrol against the building, and then set them alight with grenades. This assault was particularly daring, as the target was just a few metres from the local police station. The final raid of that long night of violence occurred in the nearby town of Cinisi. At about 3am Rosa Orlando in Serughetti was blown out of her bed by an explosion on the ground floor below, where the joint branch of the Socialist and Communist parties had its premises. Yet this building was just a few yards from a police barracks, where a guard was on night duty in the street.

In all, within the space of a few hours, six towns were attacked in western Sicily, or rather six branches of the two left-wing parties. Each group launching the attacks numbered 10 to 15 men and used cars or lorries to move around. Machine guns, petrol bombs and grenades also indicated a high level of organisation. Many of these attacks were launched by the Giuliano gang, but the Mafia was directly involved in some of them, for example in Partinico the local Mafia boss was wounded in the attack. Even if all the attackers weren't *Mafiosi*, at the very least the Mafia had to be consulted about attacks on its territory.

Very few of these crimes were ever punished. And the attacks continued. In October 1947 a Communist Party member and experienced peasant organiser, Giuseppe Maniaci, was murdered near Cinisi.

Immediately after the attack at Portella della Ginestra in May, most people instinctively blamed the Mafia. Indeed, following the attack on the Communist Party branch in Cinisi the police arrested two notorious local *Mafiosi*, Don Masi Impastato and Cesare Manzella, whom we shall meet again in the next chapter.

3

Hotel Delle Palme

After 1945 the redistribution of land and the introduction of mechanisation led to a rapid increase in unemployment in the countryside. Peasants were pushed away from infertile and poor rural areas, and pulled towards the lure of secure and well-paid employment elsewhere. Under fascism it had also been virtually forbidden to move house and change jobs, so after Mussolini's death the floodgates opened for migration.

The social consequences were enormous: in the 1950s Italy was transformed from a mainly agricultural nation into an urban society; for the first time the majority of Italians now lived in big towns or cities rather than in the countryside. The Sicilian capital Palermo saw the biggest increase in population, between 1951 and 1961 its population rose by 20 per cent, to 600,000. These new migrants needed somewhere to live, and at the same time, many of the people who until recently had been big landowners had money they needed to invest – so a building boom began.

The Mafia moved to the towns and cities too. This was where power and money were increasingly concentrated, and some of the more sophisticated *Mafiosi* saw that the building trade was an area ripe for picking. After all, both for housing and public sector works there was a great demand to invest, and at that time it was an industry which didn't require a great deal of skill.

One emblematic case was Francesco Vassallo, who began his building career by winning a contract to build new sewer systems in two fast-growing Palermo suburbs in 1951. It was odd that someone who officially defined his trade as a 'cart driver' could win such a contract, and odder still given the fact he had served three jail sentences. The key factor, which has subsequently become a typical warning sign of Mafia activity, is that all other bidders suddenly withdrew their offers. Vassallo then engaged in another classic trick; once he had won the contract, costs suddenly spiralled by 11 per cent. Two years later he was again the only contractor to put in a bid to build a school, and after the contract was signed the cost eventually increased by 70 per cent. The fact that he was able to receive billions in unsecured loans was a further sign that the Mafia was moving into the financial sector. Vassallo went on to become one of Palermo's most important builders over the next thirty years, participating in the notorious 'sack of Palermo' when the city was brutalised by unregulated building speculation.

One of the more unusual areas of Mafia interest was fishing. This was opposed by an activist who had moved to Sicily from the far north of Italy, Danilo Dolci, who helped local fishing families from Cinisi and the surrounding area to develop a campaign against illegal fishing. Not only were illegal boats unregistered, they also used explosives and fine-meshed nets that they dragged along the sea bottom, hauling in even the smallest fish and therefore jeopardising future stocks. One day a coastguard boat, with police aboard, came across some illegal fishermen who shot at them with a sub-machine gun before escaping at high speed. The response of the authorities was to withdraw the motorboat to Palermo and to transfer most of the police officers to other posts. It was the umpteenth example of collusion between the authorities and the Mafia. Naturally this demoralised the fishermen, who among other things had to pay a percentage to the Mafia for every catch they landed.

By the 1950s there was another reason for the Mafia wanting 'sea power' – drug smuggling. As early as 1952 Italian police, working with the FBI, had seized a 12-lb consignment of heroin just inland, at Alcamo, This shipment was part of an operation run by the notorious Italian-American gangster Frank 'Three Fingers' Coppola, who was arrested, along with Salvatore Greco and John Priziola, a family head from Detroit.

The real linchpin in this early period was Lucky Luciano. Born Salvatore Lucania in Sicily in 1897, he had emigrated to the US in his youth. He gained prominence under Al Capone and became boss of New York by the early 1930s through an alliance with a Jewish gangster named Meyer Lansky. The authorities finally managed to convict him of a serious crime in 1936 – running a prostitution ring – and he was given a minimum 30-year sentence. But he was suddenly released in 1946, when the head of the American navy's secret service wrote that Luciano: 'had been a great help to the armed forces' during the Second World War. There is considerable evidence to show that Luciano used his Mafia links to provide US authorities with very useful intelligence and personal contacts.

Since he had never taken out American citizenship, Luciano was deported, and arrived in Sicily in April 1947. By 1950 he was already receiving 450 kilos of industrial heroin a year from Milan, refining it, and then getting his couriers to take it across the Atlantic. The following year the FBI sent an agent named Charles Siragusa to Italy to investigate Italian–American drug traffickers; he complained to a US Senate commission a few years later that Luciano was 'the king of drug traffickers', and lamented the Italian authorities' lack of interest in Luciano's activities.

The real turning point in the drugs trade, however, took place in Palermo a few years later. The decisions made there were to have major consequences around the world.

Hotel Delle Palme

Despite its four stars, you hardly notice the Hotel Delle Palme in central Palermo, as much of its façade is covered with a thin film of soot caused by the exhaust fumes of the traffic that thunders past outside. It wasn't always like this: in the nineteenth century it was one of the most elegant villas in the city, built by the British Whitaker family with profits from the growing wine trade.

The Wagner suite on the mezzazine floor, with antique mirrors reflecting a vaulted ceiling of gilt and cerulean blue, was the venue for a four-day meeting in October 1957 that set up the basis for the modern world drugs trade. Two closely associated groups were meeting: Italian-American gangsters and the Sicilian Mafia. When they sat down, the Americans were by far the most dominant of the two, but they had several problems they needed to solve. A very vocal US senator named Estes Kefauver had recently put them in the limelight in a series of public hearings, which had also led to new anti-drug laws being passed in 1956. Moreover, the traditional entry point for drugs into the United States, Cuba, was now in a very fragile state. Batista, the dictator who ran the island, was becoming an embarrassment for the US government, which withdrew military aid in 1958. Everything changed once Fidel Castro took power in a popular revolution in January 1959.

So, despite the Italian-Americans' wealth and influence, the man who chaired the meeting, Giuseppe 'Joe Bananas' Bonanno, had some serious worries. He had been head of New York's most powerful family since 1931, but now one in three family members were under arrest on drug charges. He could count on a positive reception from his poorer Sicilian allies, especially because he had come home. Along with many Italian-American gangsters, he was born in the old country, in Castellammare del Golfo, in 1905. But as with so many, he had left for the US during the fascist period, in 1924. Soon Bonanno became 'Joe Bananas', and in the prohibition period rose quickly in Mafia ranks, organising whisky bootlegging and running speakeasies.

His emergence as the leader of one of the most important New York 'families', which took his name, occurred because he was one of the winners in the 'Castellammarese War' of 1929-31.

The undisputed winner of the war was Lucky Luciano, who set up a ruling 'Commission' of all the New York families. The Italian-American Mafia continued to modernise and look for political influence; for example, at the 1932 Democratic Party national convention in Chicago, Luciano shared a suite with leader of New York's second assembly district. Luciano, living in Naples since 1946, was at the Hotel Delle Palme as well, alongside Bonanno, his comrade in arms from the Castellammarese War.

The Sicilian Mafia had consolidated its political contacts more recently. When Mafia leader Calogero Vizzini died in 1954, the growing links between the Mafia and the Christian Democrats were revealed by the attendance at his funeral. Given that two of his brothers were priests and one was a bishop, it was not surprising that 60 clergymen came to pay their respects. However, 52 Christian Democrat MPs also attended, including five government ministers, and afterwards the local party branch was closed for a week of mourning.

The new *capo di tutti i capi*, Giuseppe Genco Russo, attended the meeting, but he really didn't count for much in Palermo. Having said that, he was certainly big in his hometown of Mussomeli, high up in central Italy. He owned large areas of land, was a major shareholder in a bank, and had an influential role as a member of the Christian Democrat Party. Now aged 64, he was very much a representative of the old rural Mafia, as he still kept his mule inside his house and had an outside toilet. Overall, Sicilian *Mafiosi* were the junior partners at the summit – yet over the next two decades they would slowly rise to dominate the alliance.

Collectively, the people who sat down together in the Wagner suite had spent hundreds of years in prison, been convicted or acquitted of dozens of murders and were frequently talked about in the press. Everybody knew who they were, furthermore the meeting wasn't secret since the Americans checked in using their US passports. Under Italian law, hotels have [they still do today] to provide lists of residents to the local police immediately, and this was done. Indeed the police officer at the 'foreigners' desk', Lo Piccolo, sent a note to Palermo police HQ telling them the head of the American Mafia was in town. The same day he told them that Genco Russo, along with 'twelve unknowns', were meeting with the Americans. The police didn't move a muscle, neither then nor over the next three days of the summit, and they only told Interpol about the meeting nine months later. Although they sent an officer named Malannino to hang around the hotel bar, the meeting was allowed to go ahead.

In essence the Americans wanted the Sicilians to help solve their problems. The people from the old country were willing, had considerable skills and many of them were unknown to the US police. As an 'offshore' base it might be much further away than Cuba, but similar conditions existed in Sicily – a lenient police force and a working relationship with the main party of government. For this alliance to work, though, the Sicilians needed to organise themselves differently. They needed to leave their origins of being parasites on the rural economy behind them once and for all, and become international investors. In economic terms they had to become capitalists, linked to operations in three continents. Capital needed to be accumulated to invest in transport and buy raw materials, and areas for diversification and investment had to be found to reinvest the huge amounts of money that would be made. None of this could be done by men who still kept their mules on the ground floor of their houses. Given their long experience in the heart of the capitalist beast, the Americans understood that they needed to nurture a young generation of murderous entrepreneurs.

Most of this was discussed at a more private affair separate to the summit, an interminably long dinner at Spano's restaurant on the Palermo sea front. Lucky Luciano and 'Joe Bananas' had invited some of the young Turks to join them. These included 29-year-old Tommaso Buscetta from Palermo, 34-year-old Salvatore 'Little Bird' Greco from the Palermo suburb of Ciaculli, and Gaetano Badalamenti from Cinisi, also 34. Bonanno told the Sicilians that they needed to set up a 'Commission' so that things could run smoothly – the Americans had suffered a long and costly history of gang wars. The Commission's function would not be the creation of a mini Mafia parliament that centralised all activities, but a body that set the ground rules that allowed each local gang to prosper. A lot was at stake: millions could be made, but those taking part also risked long prison sentences.

The time was ripe for the Americans' plan. Besides, many doors were still wide open. In 1959 the New York office of the FBI had 400 officers investigating communism, and just four dealing with organised crime. The Commission would provide the framework for *Mafiosi* to become global criminals.

Towns like Cinisi, to the west of Palermo, were ideal for transporting drugs to the United States – up to 80 per cent of the inhabitants had relatives across the Atlantic. To all intents and purposes, a visit to relatives was perfectly legitimate. Furthermore, many Mafia bosses had lived in America for many years, including Cinisi godfather 'Don' Cesare Manzella.

By the time he moved back to Cinisi from the US in 1946 Manzella had made large sums of money and began to play the role of a benefactor of charities, a man who resolved family disputes, or in other words a 'man of honour'. Gaspare Cucinella, a post-office worker and amateur actor, remembers him well and agrees – sarcastically – with the stereotypical role he played: 'Don Cesare Manzella was the town's benefactor, he'd been in America, everybody would kiss his hand – "all the best, Don Cesare" – that was the environment you lived in. There was nothing else.'

As a supposed 'man of honour', Cucinella continues, 'it was as if he was everybody's relative, he was related to all of us'. And, given the strength of family ties, Manzella felt he had the right to interfere in the most intimate areas of people's lives. Cucinella remembers: 'When I got engaged, her parents didn't want her to marry me – and it ended up with Don Cesare Manzella getting involved: "Do you really need to marry this woman?", he said. "Why don't you just leave her alone and mind your own business?"' This is typical Mafia behaviour and language. Vague and indirect questions are asked about the consequences of not giving the answer that is expected – in other words they are threats. Cucinella was one of the few who threw them back in Manzella's face: 'So I answered: "What's all this got to do with you? Why don't you mind your own bloody business? And in the meantime, I'll mind my own." He just walked away, laughing.'

Manzella still visited the States very often, and was making huge profits in the emerging drugs trade. As early as 1958 a police report described him as follows:

> He is the Mafia boss of Cinisi, and has a domineering and violent personality . . . Cesare Manzella is cunning, with remarkable organisational abilities . . . Such is his influence that the crimes committed by his accomplices are not even reported to the authorities. For this reason . . . he has always escaped justice, in fact he has no convictions. He makes use of hit-men for murders . . . It is beyond doubt, however, that the small number of serious crimes which have taken place in the Cinisi area were decided by him. There is no other explanation: a Mafia boss such as Manzella would not allow illegal acts to take place in his territory without his permission . . . Manzella himself is very well-off economically, being the owner of substantial real estate (olive groves, market gardens, buildings, all within Cinisi), valued at about 20 million lire.

The drugs trade was starting to make Mafia bosses very rich. The 20 million lire mentioned in this 1958 report is worth about £300 million today. People like Manzella were no longer simply parasites organising low-level protection rackets in the countryside. They were international businessmen, albeit of an unusual kind.

The whole town was frightened of them. People in Cinisi weren't afraid because they were cowards, but for a reason that this report could never mention: as a rich and powerful man Manzella had a lot of influence, in essence he was protected by members of the police and local politicians. If honest people were to stand up against the Mafia, they knew that not only were local politicians and policemen unlikely to protect them, but in some cases they would actively take the Mafia's side. That's why, as the report states, so many crimes went unreported.

This local power structure produces public grovelling, a reality in which people feel obliged to demonstrate their lack of self-respect publicly. A Communist activist from this period remembers: 'As soon as Cesare Manzella arrived in the town square it was all "Don Cesare, Don Cesare" - people kissing his hand.' This was a perfectly normal event at this time. In the nearby town of Carini another young Communist remembers 'his' Mafia boss thus: 'He used to walk up and down with the mayor, the priest, the police superintendent - people used to kiss his hand, and so on.'

Cesare Manzella and the 'First Mafia War'

Despite the existence of the Commission, and the fact that Manzella's deputy in Cinisi, Gaetano Badalamenti, was one of its three members, the massive and sudden increase in wealth and influence caused by the drugs trade created instability. To finance big drug deals individual Mafia families had to make agreements with other gangs, they had to trust each other and make huge financial investments on trust - a problematic situation that quickly brings to mind the phrase 'there's no honour among thieves'. Perhaps this was what Mafia leader Giuseppe Genco Russo meant at the Hotel Delle Palme summit in 1957, in the only snippet of conversation that was overheard: 'when a hundred dogs are fighting over a bone, blessed be the man who is far away'. In any event, it was a major drug deal that was to be Manzella's undoing.

In February 1962 Manzella, together with other gang leaders Salvatore Greco and the brothers Angelo and Salvatore La Barbera, raised the money to buy a large consignment of heroin. Delivery to the United States was entrusted to Manzella's gang, but when the heroin got to America less money came back than had been agreed. The Americans said they had paid for the amount they received. The La Barbera brothers suspected that Manzella's man had kept some of the heroin.

It was a large amount of money. Since the Hotel Delle Palme summit five years earlier the price of heroin had nearly doubled in New York, from $12,000 to $22,000 a kilo. The Sicilians were selling it on at four or five times the price they paid, and by 1963 Sicily had become the world's largest staging area for drugs. The Mafia could no longer turn back: the drugs trade had become vital to the activities of many gangs and members. Given these serious accusations and the essential nature of the drugs trade itself, the Commission held a summit, where it was agreed that Manzella and his accomplices were not to blame.

But the La Barberas didn't agree, and decided to launch the 'First Mafia War'. It began in December when the man who had taken the consignment to the US, and other gang members, were killed in Palermo. This was a very serious move. These were attacks on another major gang and against the Commission. Salvatore La Barbera, who had taken part in the summit but ignored its outcome, was challenging the whole way the Mafia operated. This was why, three weeks later, he left home and never came back.

The La Barberas started to hit back at the loss of one of their leaders. Early on the morning of 26 April 1963 Cesare Manzella and his estate manager Filippo Vitale were driving through their lemon groves when they saw a car identical to Badalamenti's. Confused, they got out, but were then blown up by a massive car bomb that was heard throughout Cinisi. The police officers who arrived at the scene later wrote in their report:

spread over the ground one could notice metal parts belonging to the vehicle, together with shreds of human remains and burnt clothing.

Seventeen metres from the crater were the smoking remains of the front end of the vehicle; and at 28 metres the remains of a human pelvis together with a right leg missing its lower extremities. Fifteen metres away there was a pistol, around which there were other human remains, including a severed but intact human head. On the branch of a walnut tree there were the remains of a dark grey pair of trousers, in the back pocket of which there was a wallet containing 27,000 lire and some sheets of paper with notes written on them.

In one of these notes Manzella had written down the address of one of Luciano Leggio's gang from Corleone – the top Mafia leader at the time, who was also in alliance with Manzella – as well as the car registration number of La Barbera's top killer. The La Barberas had got to Manzella first, yet despite all his notoriety Manzella died without ever being convicted of a single crime.

The killing continued. Two months later Angelo La Barbera was attacked and riddled with six bullets, but somehow he survived. Significantly, he wasn't attacked on the 'mean streets' of Palermo but at the other end of Italy – in Milan – the country's financial capital. Clearly, the Mafia was no longer just something local, confined to small Sicilian towns.

When the dust settled, it became clear that Manzella's death had produced three changes. The first took a few years to have an effect. One of the mourners at Manzella's funeral was a 15-year-old boy named Peppino Impastato, who was taken along by his mother, and who was deeply shocked by the death of Manzella, his uncle. The second immediate consequence was that Manzella's right-hand man, Gaetano Badalamenti, became the new Mafia boss in Cinisi.

Then something completely unexpected happened, and produced the third change. On 7 July a car bomb was planted in the town of Ciaculli as part of this gang war; the intended targets were probably Salvatore Greco and Luciano Leggio. But the bombers partly bungled the operation and the police were called to investigate. When one of them opened the boot a huge explosion rocked the whole area. Flames shot fifty feet into the air, a nearby villa was totally destroyed, and seven policemen were literally blown to pieces.

The media and the government were now driven into action. A permanent parliamentary committee was set up, the Anti-Mafia commission, and 2,000 arrest warrants were issued, including ones for Tommaso Buscetta and Badalamenti. Both went on the run: Badalamenti may have been one of the Mafia's top three, but now he had to learn fast how to be invisible, even to his own organisation. For the foreseeable future there was to be no more Commission, no more regional meetings, no 'boss of bosses'. From 1963 to the end of the decade it was 'every man for himself', or more precisely every local gang for itself.

But who was Badalamenti, the new boss in Cinisi and one of three most powerful members of the Mafia?

4

The Man Who Made Leaves Move

During his most difficult trial, an American lawyer once said of 'Don Tano', an abbreviation of Gaetano Badalamenti: 'There are three things guaranteed in life – death, taxes and Badalamenti's silence.' Facing a life sentence in the 'Pizza Connection' trial, 63-year-old Badalamenti refused to plead guilty to a minor charge, and imposed the same response on his son Vito and many other relatives. When one of his co-defendants started to break ranks, Badalamenti ominously warned him: 'if you take this plea, you're out of the family'.

Families are hugely important to Italians, both in the north of the country, and in the deep south such as Sicily – they are probably the strongest organising bond in Italian society. Being part of a family is almost like being a soldier in an army: your life is not your own. Although many Italians go through family life happily, the rhythm of their lives is often dictated by the marriages, deaths, birthdays, births, illnesses, graduations, engagements of many of their close relatives, not to mention the rituals of Easter, Christmas and New Year. Due respect has to be shown at all times. Once you get married – and still today the traditional view is that there must be something a bit wrong with unmarried people – your family duties almost doubled because you now have obligations towards your spouse's family too.

At the head of any traditional family is the patriarch, the father. Italians have a useful expression for describing his power – *padre padrone* – literally 'boss father'. When this widespread mentality is then reproduced within a Mafia gang, which is normally based on blood ties, the power of the leader becomes virtually absolute. A woman who married into the Badalamenti clan noticed the tradition and hierarchy at weddings and christenings: 'All the men are on one side of the room, all the women are on the other. The women who never talk but know everything sit near the men, whereas the younger or more stupid women sit further away.' This was how she saw things being organised:

> A Mafia family is organised like a beehive. First of all there's the queen bee, the boss, then come the drones, the soldiers, then the worker bees – generally the women or men who are distant relatives. Women can only marry men approved by the queen bee, there's no getting away from that. But in a way women have an easier life because their husbands always have to show them respect.

The claustrophobic power of family ties is magnified in towns such as Cinisi because almost everybody is related to many other people – even second or third cousins are important links. Letterboxes are dominated by just a few surnames: Badalamenti, Bartolotta, Impastato, Mangiapane, Maniaci, Manzella, Palazzolo, Ruvolo and Vitale.

Another very strong characteristic of Cinisi is the use of nicknames, which often help in distinguishing people with identical names. The one used for the Badalamenti clan began one day when an ancestor of Don Tano decided he wanted to be noticed, so he put huge cow bells on his livestock to make sure everybody would notice it was his cattle that were passing by – indeed, cattle were the family's main source of income. And that became the family's nickname: 'cow bells'.

The Badalamenti clan is descended from two patriarch brothers, Vito and Salvatore, both of whom had cattle herds and sired many children. Gaetano, as the song that introduces *The Sopranos* television series says, was 'born under a bad sign' in 1923, in the sense that his father died the same year. While he may not have 'got himself a gun' straight away, he grew up in a violent town, with his four older brothers getting involved in various kinds of crime before him. He went to school for four years, but at the age of 10 he started work in the family business.

His parents were respected locally, although not in the way he later became. Someone who married into the family remembers the reason for that respect: 'both because they were experts in choosing cattle and because their cheeses were the best. All this was due to their skill in preparing the cheese, as well as their knowledge of when to move their cattle – from the coast to the mountains and vice versa – therefore their milk was always the best.'

One of the main reasons for Don Tano's early success was cattle rustling, for which the 18-year-old Gaetano was first reported in 1941. Cattle rustling might seem quaint and low-level criminal activity to most, but at that time it was an important crime. People were so poor – or supplies were so scarce – that a few aspirin tablets could be exchanged for several fish or hens. The theft, or killing, of even a single cow was a serious economic blow to a family.

Another of his early activities was robbing houses, often with another young sidekick, Procopio Di Maggio. One of their favourite targets was young women's dowries, the luxurious presents families collected for many years in expectation of a daughter's marriage. All of these criminal activities, whether it was cattle rustling or burglary, were taking place in a small town where news travels fast. And to a large extent, a professional criminal wants his reputation to be known far and wide, so word spread very quickly about their actions.

Although Gaetano Badalamenti did not come from a strictly Mafia background, after the Second World War his family links read like a Mafia family tree. His wife, Teresa

Vitale, is from nearby Castellammare del Golfo, a key town in terms of links with the US. One of her sisters is married to Filippo Rimi, of the powerful Alcamo Mafia; that marriage made Badalamenti and Filippo Rimi cousins. In turn, his cousins from Alcamo were linked with the Bonannos in New York, his sons-in-law with the Maggadinos of Buffalo. The clan was clearly international. Indeed, for a long period one of Gaetano's brothers, Emanuele, virtually commuted from Cinisi to Detroit – there was a jumbo jet a week from the local airport. Many of Badalamenti's relatives worked at the airport, and when drug smuggling got big it was often they who would load and unload all the baggage, drugs and dollars. In its heyday there were about 200 people in the Badalamenti clan, who managed to move about a thousand foot soldiers, *picciotti*. It was something more than a family; it was an organisation, often prepared to use force.

Badalamenti's first arrest in 1946, for criminal association and conspiracy to kidnap, showed that he had started out on a professional criminal career. He often boasted with *Mafiosi* that once he had been 'made' and joined the Mafia – soon after Lucky Luciano's arrival in Naples in 1946 – he was entrusted with his first murder. Luciano had been slapped at the Agnano racecourse, just outside the city, and Badalamenti's job was to organise the murder of this offender, which he entrusted to a local criminal, Salvatore Zaza.

Looking back now, Gaetano Badalmenti was just one small-time criminal out of many. The only law these people followed was that of the jungle, and Badalamenti – through chance or luck – managed to survive. Many of his actions were low-level feuds if judged by the standards under which *Mafiosi* were operating by the 1960s, but murder was murder whatever the year. In June 1947 he was first accused of killing someone, but when the charge was made he was already on the run.

Four months later something more serious happened, indicating a real battle for power, and therefore a real growth in local Mafia gangs. A few years before, the Badalamentis and another local family had had a serious disagreement.

The arrival of a senior Italian-American gangster led to the decision that the other gang had to make a sacrifice to the Badalamentis, or in other words one of them had to die. Understandably, the poor man in question, Procopio Finazzo, shut himself in at home and virtually never came out, even though he was a good shot. On 10 October 1946 he did emerge, and Badalamenti managed to wound him. Exactly a year later Finazzo went to a bar for a drink. Coming out, he saw six men waiting for him in the main square, he begged the barman to lend him a gun but was cut down immediately. This time, Badalamenti faced a charge of organising the murder. This was a sure sign that he was becoming important – ordering six other people to murder on his behalf shows that there was an organisation, and that Badalamenti had power within it.

The charges mounted up. In 1949 another arrest warrant was issued for kidnapping and extortion, but Badalamenti was now far away. The same year he left Italy illegally for Detroit, but was deported in 1950. His brother Emanuele, 20 years older than Gaetano, had already moved to the US and ended up running a supermarket and petrol station in Monroe, Michigan. Back in Cinisi the following year, Gaetano was arrested for kidnapping but released without charge.

Two years later he was again arrested for cigarette smuggling and armed resistance to arrest, but charges were dropped, this time for lack of evidence. Three years after that he was apprehended once more, again with a weapon, but this time in possession of 3,000 kilos of foreign cigarettes. Cigarette smuggling is still a key activity for organised crime today, and the system tends to work like this. Senior criminals make perfectly legal deals with major cigarette manufacturers to deliver massive amounts of cigarettes to a third country. In turn these items are then taken to sea and unloaded from cargo ships onto speedboats just outside Italian territorial waters, and then the illegal cargo speeds to land and is distributed up and down the country, although mainly in the south. The reason is that the government has a monopoly on cigarette sales in Italy and imposes a huge duty on top of the manufacturers' prices. Once the price of duty is avoided, these cigarettes can be sold for close to half the legal price, all the while guaranteeing big profits for the criminal gangs that distribute them.

Far greater profits could be made dealing in drugs rather than cigarettes. In 1951 an American police report named Badalamenti as one of the people involved in sending a 50-kilo consignment of heroin to the US. The following year an Italian police investigation states that he was involved in a drug smuggling ring with other top criminals, such as Frank Coppola. One of the ways that drugs were moved was through the easy access to fruit and vegetable markets in both the US and Italy. Police eventually discovered a 'drugged oranges' trade in 1959; drugs were injected into the base of oranges, thus doubling their weight and making them 'pregnant' until their 'birth' on the other side of the Atlantic. This system was virtually global: the raw material was shipped from Syria and Turkey to the Sicilian coasts, where the speedboats sometimes used for illegal fishing brought it ashore and into citrus groves. Then certain oranges were injected, placed in crates, and sent on to Palermo for export. The other up-and-coming *Mafioso* in Cinisi, Procopio Di Maggio, had links with other *Mafiosi* who had also been at the Hotel Delle Palme summit, so a completely alternative route existed as well.

Although Badalamenti had already been arrested and charged several times, he was yet to spend a long time in jail. Not only were the police aware of his charmed life, but local people too had started to realise he was close to being untouchable. In 1957 he was believed to have stolen five head of cattle from one family, and 13 from another. These actions probably weren't directly important from a financial point of view, but their purpose was probably broader: to show people who was in charge. Gaspare Cucinella recalls an event from the same period: 'One day, for some reason or other, he wanted to show he was boss of the whole town. So he took all his cows down into town and let them drink from the fountain outside the town hall. Nobody said a word against him.' Not for nothing did an Anti-Mafia Commission report comment years later: 'Due to the iron law of silence in this situation, out of fear of even worse reprisals, injured parties sometimes do not even report crimes. In any event, they never voice their suspicions.' This is why, a year after the 1957 Hotel Delle Palme summit, a police headquarters report could say of Badalamenti: 'due to his past and his violence he represents an important figure in the local underworld. So much so that local people fear him to the extent that they prefer to silently accept his bullying and crimes due to their fear of vendettas and retaliation.'

Once again, individual words are important: Badalamenti isn't defined as being a member of the Mafia but of the underworld. Decades were to pass before membership of the Mafia was made a criminal offence; decades were to pass too before a verdict was reached in a courtroom that an organisation known as the Mafia even existed. In a notorious case in 1975, a Communist politician had accused a former Christian Democrat mayor of Palermo of being a *Mafioso*, the mayor had then sued for libel. During the hearing, when the defence lawyer asked the former mayor whether he was a *Mafioso* or not, the judge ruled the question out of order. There was a criminal conspiracy amongst the powerful, not only in a legal sense, but also in a political and moral sense, to keep all of this quiet – often because these influential people had links with top gang leaders or were prepared to come to an arrangement with them sometimes, particularly during elections if they were politicians.

So, legally it was as a simple criminal, rather than as a *Mafioso*, that Badalamenti continued his life of crime. In September 1961 two murders were committed in Cinisi, and it was widely believed Badalamenti was responsible for them – the two victims were viewed as being 'guilty' of getting ideas above their station. But once again Badalamenti wasn't convicted. Unusually for a mere cattle farmer, he now owned a car, in which, according to the police: 'he often travels from one town to another committing all kinds of crimes, thus becoming one of the most influential and dangerous members of the Cinisi underworld'.

The following month the police reported that Badalamenti had met top Mafia leaders at Palermo Airport, and in

February 1962 he was again spotted by the police at a Mafia summit in Rome. The new airport, opened in 1960, was within Cinisi's council boundaries, and in later years became a Badalamenti stronghold. His family owned a nearby mountain that was the only local source of rock, gravel and sand in the area, and very quickly Don Tano came to own two construction companies, a concrete factory and fleet of lorries. The authorities believed Badalamenti was coordinating links between the Sicilian and American Mafias, yet despite all of this he was convicted of hardly any of the crimes for which he was arrested and charged. Local people saw that he lived a charmed life, that he was untouchable.

His influence and eyes must have been everywhere; indeed, his black eyes burned like lumps of coal. As somebody once said of him: 'In Cinisi a leaf didn't move without Don Tano knowing about it.' Photographs from back then show him often dressing as a typical peasant, in an ordinary jacket and cloth cap, although on special occasions he wore a suit and sunglasses. Over the years his face became burnt by the sun and grizzled, like that of most Sicilians – yet this was a man who operated on a global scale. His behaviour in public, particularly at trials, was both courteous and grave, he acted like a real 'man of honour'. His measured response to any question or comment, often answered indirectly, meant that people hung on his every word, simply because they knew how powerful he was.

But when his boss Cesare Manzella was blown up in 1963 during the First Mafia War, the leaves stopped moving. Badalamenti went on the run for six years and disappeared from his hometown.

5

It's in the Air that You Breathe

Fifteen miles to the west of Palermo, the town of Cinisi is like many in Sicily: small, isolated and – particularly in the summer heat – sleepy. Like other towns it is also claustrophobic, everybody knows everybody else, and everybody often knows everybody else's business. People talk, maybe not in front of you, but they talk. You sense it when you're walking along the streets, in the way people look at you. Some give you friendly glances if you know them, others greet you in an apparently friendly way, but you can see a knowing or penetrating look in their eyes.

If people don't know you then their gaze is even more inquisitive, searching and invariably hostile. If you're an outsider arriving by car, by the time you've locked the door many people have registered your alien presence. All of this surveying happens from two vantage points: people looking out from shops or at tables outside of bars, or in hot weather people sitting on chairs on their doorsteps. You are being watched all the time, there is no escape from the equivalent of hundreds of 'smart' CCTV cameras. Even houses with closed doors can be observation posts: you can easily imagine people peering at you from between the slats of their window blinds.

Lots of communication takes place without words, as one Cinisi resident put it: 'Our culture is one in which nobody talks but everybody knows everything. It's as if there are some magnetic waves.' Everyday activity is often highly symbolic. Because everybody knows everything, you know that one supermarket is run by a *Mafioso* and one isn't. The same goes for the butcher, or the petrol station, or the numerous bars on the main street.

Felicetta Vitale's family has been running a bar on the main street for nearly fifty years. Things haven't changed very much from the 1960s and 1970s she remembers:

> Back then every bar had its own clientele: there was the Bar Palazzolo on the corner of the town square – that was the bar for the 'gentlemen' of· the town. The Bar Roma was across the street, and it was the students' bar. Halfway down there were another two bars, one in front of the other. One was the Maltese, which was used by cattle farmers, whereas opposite it, the Mastrominico – which has now become a pub – was used by building workers and manual labourers. Right at the bottom there were another two bars which were frequented by truck drivers, since they were very close to the main road.
>
> This was how the town was divided: these were your reference points. However, over time two groups – workers and students – started to mingle.

The town has always been divided, but the walls and fences are in people's minds. If a member of a Mafia family gets a top-up for their mobile from a non-Mafia shop it's a significant event. Maybe they're making a statement, or sending a message – but what is it? Is it friendly or aggressive? Alternatively, if a non-Mafia man suddenly goes for a drink in a Mafia bar he doesn't make that move by chance, he has a very good reason and will set people wondering why he has broken the habits of a lifetime.

Growing up in Sicily, people understand what talking to *Mafiosi* can lead to. According to Giuseppe Nobile from the nearby town of Partinico, this means that the underlying meaning of communication between ordinary people and a Mafia family can be the complete opposite of what it appears to be:

> People's common sense is not to criticise them publicly, but to keep well away from them. This is the average way of thinking for ordinary Sicilians, poor Sicilians. You try to keep as far away from them as possible, because getting involved with them socially or economically only creates problems.
>
> Formally, the normal behaviour of ordinary people is one of extreme respect, without ever challenging their social authority. For example, if a *Mafioso* is arrested and his wife is left on her own, when her next-door neighbour meets her she will express her sympathy, her understanding. But she is going through the motions, she doesn't really feel like this. If he's really in serious trouble you show all the sympathy in the world, but underneath you're happy.

Even a simple gesture like saying hello to people is a minefield; just by greeting a *Mafioso* you can risk being sucked into their web. By saying hello to someone you know – a perfectly normal thing to do – you are sending a message to that person and to anyone else who sees that gesture. A *Mafioso* may then want to develop that relationship. So the next time he might stop for a chat, the third time offer to buy you a coffee in a bar. At that point a threshold is crossed, but not only that of a bar. You have accepted that person up until then, said hello to him, chatted together, there is no reason in the world why you shouldn't have a drink with him. But that level of friendship means something, and its existence is noted by many others. You can't deny it, nor say it was imposed on you – you are now friends with this person.

The way a long-time opponent of the Mafia, Piero Impastato, puts it, is that: 'The Mafia wants to create consensus. It wants everybody to say hello to each other, so we're all in things together. It's as if Cinisi is the sea, and they're fish swimming around in it.' In a way, the Mafia wants to create the illusion that there are no divisions, that everybody shares the same traditional values of family and religion.

The Mafia wants to embody society's traditions and show its members as generous and caring people. To do this, the society they live in has to accept them and not ostracise them. This is why getting people to say hello to them is important. Piero recalls how his relative and Mafia patriarch used to behave: 'Don Masi Impastato always used to watch you when you saw him, to see whether you said hello or not. If you didn't you were rude, a bad person, if you did you were a good guy – but it was always down to you to make the first move.' What these behavioural patterns reveal is the mental discipline imposed, as well as a broad social conditioning. But there is also the more subtle mechanism by which the Mafia are trying to dictate everyday social activities.

Once you've started acknowledging *Mafiosi*, the only way back is to suddenly start completely ignoring them. But exactly when do you start doing that? And what do you do if you're with your mother and she says hello to a *Mafioso*?

Giovanni Impastato, one of two brothers who are central to this whole story, remembers his early years in Cinisi thus: 'Growing up as a kid you just breathed Mafia. I played with relatives of Procopio Di Maggio and many other *Mafiosi*. But later on we each made our own choices and went our separate ways.' Pino Manzella, another man who started to oppose the Mafia in the 1960s, points out the difficulty of completely keeping your distance if a town is dominated by *Mafiosi*: 'For many years I never said hello to these kinds of people. But, after while, you end up ignoring nearly everyone!' It is so difficult to make a break because to be surrounded by the Mafia in towns such as Cinisi is normal: 'When you're growing up in a town like this you simply come across the Mafia because it's in the air that you breathe.'

Cinisi

The central focus of Cinisi, if it has one, is the town hall and the small square outside it. The building is a former monastery, but more than anything else the town is shaped by the main street, Corso Umberto I. Named after King Humbert I, it is normally abbreviated to Corso; it is the only wide street in the town, and like most others, it runs down from the high part of the town towards the sea. Like some streets in capital cities – such as O'Connell Street in Dublin – it is where all of the most major events have taken place.

What happens and who you see on the Corso depends on the time of day. At about 8am men start to appear and slowly congregate in groups. They are either elderly, that is pensioners, or younger and unemployed. In essence they have been chucked out of the house until lunchtime so women can do the cleaning and cooking. It gets busier as the shops open, and you start to see more women, either shopping or serving customers. The street bustles until 1pm and then suddenly empties. It's lunchtime: the shop shutters are pulled down and people go home to eat and snooze, and nothing much happens until about 4pm. By this time people who work in the public sector have finished work, and they are joined by others who work outside town. So there are another three or four hours of activity until the shops shut again, but after that the Corso is dotted by groups of teenagers for another three hours – bored just as teenagers get bored in any other town in the world. And just as in any other main street, they watch enviously as big cars and motorcycles drive by.

As you walk up the Corso, your eyes are naturally drawn upwards, to the end – the council building housed in the former monastery. Just above it, closing in your vision, are two mountain slopes that sweep down in a V-shape. Depending on the time of year, if you look in that direction early in the morning you're blinded, as the sun rises from behind one of the mountains. But if you're going down the Corso towards the sea you're sometimes faced with a peculiar sight: aircraft passing from right to left, lifting off into the air at a point that looks like the end of the street. This is Palermo Airport: first opened with two runways in 1960, followed by a third in 1968; it falls within the northern part of Cinisi's municipal boundaries.

The back streets of town, off the Corso, are claustrophobic. Not only are they very narrow, but they are arranged in a block pattern, so each corner is totally blind and you never know who is about to come round the next one. Apart from the council building and a couple of nondescript churches the town can justifiably be called ugly. In a desperate attempt at giving itself some airs and graces, halfway along the Corso there is a crossroads locally called *I quattro canti* – the four corners. This is named after a huge baroque road junction in the centre of Palermo, full of ornate statues; in Cinisi it is just another anonymous and ugly street corner like another, blink and you'd miss it.

This feeling of being hemmed in comes above all from natural rather than human geography. At the lower end of the town there are fields leading down to the sea, thus cutting the town off definitively. But at the upper end Cinisi comes to an abrupt end with Mount Pecoraro, which rises almost vertically to 3,000 feet. Throughout the day the bare rock changes colour, from light blue to gold, turning pink at sunset. When it is cloudy, if there are fluffy white clouds the mountains can seem like some inviting 'never never land'. Dark clouds, and a dark sea, make things much more threatening. Yet it is always there, brooding, emphasising the lack of an exit route. A further human barrier was erected when the motorway was built at the bottom of the mountain's slopes, yet another obstacle to moving out of town easily. The only clear open access is to the south, away from Palermo.

Although there are indications that its history goes much further back, Cinisi was really put on the map in 1617, when Benedictine monks decided to build a monastery in this largely deserted area. Cinisi was unusual in that it developed far later than similar towns nearby: in 1853 it still had only 5,269 inhabitants.

The early development of industry in nearby Palermo in the first half of the nineteenth century saw virtually no inhabitants from Cinisi taking part. When feudalism was abolished in 1812 the local order of Benedictine monks sold large areas of land immediately, because they were afraid it would be seized by the new government. The buyers were mostly notaries, although there were also a few doctors and lawyers – but with these kinds of people buying it was clear there was still no local industrial or business development. The land had not been cared for by the monks and had become impoverished with serious long-term consequences; they had frequently cut down and not replaced trees, which they sold as firewood.

The new council administration functioned well enough, but the Sicilian press did not deem political life in Cinisi worthy of any comment. In some ways sitting on the council was like belonging to a gentlemen's club: only those with high personal incomes were allowed to hold office. So, not surprisingly, it seems that virtually nobody from the town joined Garibaldi's revolutionary conquest of Sicily, leading to the creation of the Italian nation in 1860. The town elders, meanwhile, did wake up and fight to get a railway station built in Cinisi rather than in nearby Terrasini. But its opening in 1880 did not really change very much, although limited mains water supplies were developed just before the end of the century, and some electric street lighting was installed during the First World War.

There was another system of power in the area that was far more dynamic – violent criminals. This kind of lawlessness existed before the Mafia, but the same conditions applied: given that these were small towns in isolated areas that didn't produce very much wealth, the new government really wasn't that interested what happened there. So 'law and order' was pretty much a 'hit or miss' affair.

A local priest, Vito Mangiapani, wrote a book about the town in 1910 and reported: 'The most common crimes are thefts in the fields and illegal grazing, which could be stopped by creating a better system of field guards. Cattle rustling is common, as is damage to private property caused by personal hatred and vendettas.' What he may or may not have known is that these armed field guards were the people who were evolving into *Mafiosi*. These individuals, who earned money through instilling fear in people on behalf of local landowners, very quickly saw the sense of doing the same on their own behalf.

The rich people of Cinisi, the town councillors, tried to protect themselves from this lawlessness by setting up their own system of armed guards, paying their wages out of council funds – or in other words from people's taxes. The consequences were very serious: most of those hired already had criminal records, so in the long term the creation of a Mafia-type environment was only encouraged by local politicians. Furthermore, only the very rich were protected, while smaller businessmen and shopowners found criminals swarming around them to an even greater extent, and at the bottom of the pile ordinary working people were disgusted at the reality of the new 'democratic' Italian state.

The vast majority of local people were poor peasants who worked up to 16 hours a day, lived in crowded rented houses and ate meat just a handful of times a year. They don't feature in the history books for this period, although the authorities were quick to remember them during the First World War, when hundreds left town to go and fight high up in the Alps on the Austrian border. About a hundred died in such an alien environment, and roughly the same number were seriously wounded. All told, it is not surprising that when they came back, once it was clear most of them would not find work, they either emigrated or were tempted by a life of crime.

Economically speaking, the existence of Mafia gangs discourages development, as they are essentially parasitic upon others' work. They rake in money for doing and creating nothing, while at the same time demanding money from people trying to generate greater economic growth and employment. A member of a well-off and industrious family remembers problems back in the 1950s: 'We had 15 or 16 workers, back then this was a big workplace. And we were very rich. But what do you do when they kidnap your cart and driver? You might get the cart back empty, but what about the driver? They fired machine guns at our premises, they tried to kidnap my brother when he was seven.' All of this explains why you only find Mafia in poor areas, and why a hundred years ago a priest could write: 'where bad faith and fraud continue, they block the union of capital'. Not surprisingly, there were no private companies in town.

Local people with time and money to spare would pass the time of day in their own clubs, often watching other people pass by. As the parish priest wrote, for them: 'life goes on just as it did a century ago'. The most prestigious meeting place was the Circolo dei Galantuomini (Gentlemen's Club), frequented by the rich and professional people. For the middle class – small landowners and shopkeepers – there was the Circolo dei Cacciatori (Hunters' Club). The basis of membership – enough money to buy rifles and ammunition, and the free time to enjoy them – excluded poorer people. Below this was the Circolo dei Vaccari (Herdsmens' Club), for the surprisingly large number of people who grazed cattle. The meeting place of the poor was the street corner.

One inhabitant of Cinisi recalls the Gentlemen's Club thus: 'There was a big entrance room with lots of armchairs, from which you could look outside. Once in a while they went in the countryside, but they never worked.' Undoubtedly this was true, but this club was also a kind of seat of power: 'The mayors who were elected all came from these clubs, it was always the same people.'

World Wars and Mafia Wars

In Cinisi there is one word you hear a lot – *ammazzarono*. Literally it means 'they murdered' but it's used on its own, ungrammatically. It is a stark statement, describing an all too familiar event.

The cosy life for the town's elite was shattered after the end of the First World War. For a start, there was a huge

Mafia turf war in the Cinisi area – *ammazzarono* – which seemed to be driven more by a series of personal vendettas than a steady build-up in wealth and power which is the normal circumstance in which middle-ranking *Mafiosi* are tempted to launch a bid to become top dog. However the number of murders, about thirty, showed that local gangs had become sizeable. This wave of violence quickly receded due to two factors. Firstly, mass migration to the United States drained the lifeblood out of some gangs, as well as reducing the root causes of family vendettas. Secondly, the advent of a fascist dictatorship in 1922 meant that for the first time the government took public order seriously; the totalitarian ideology of fascism could not tolerate any kind of alternative power structure.

On his first visit to Sicily in 1924 Mussolini was enraged when on a trip to Piana degli Albanesi the local Mafia boss insisted he get rid of his bodyguards as he was now a guest under the Mafia's protection. Soon after that Mussolini appointed Cesare Mori, a tough no-nonsense career politician who had been fighting the Mafia since 1903, and entrusted him with full powers.

Mori quickly began a policy of mass round-ups in many Sicilian towns, a kind of collective punishment that effectively put the entire population under siege. Felicia Bartolotta, a teenager at the time, remembers what Mori – nicknamed the 'Iron Prefect' – did when he wanted to capture *Mafiosi*: 'Everybody had animals, so he cut off the water and the animals died – people had to give themselves up! Or they'd arrest women, and when the men-folk came out they were taken away.' The outcome was that many low-level members were convicted and received prison sentences, whereas more important *Mafiosi* either left the country, joined the Fascist Party or simply went dormant.

According to the new mayor, by 1927 the town's problems had been solved because everybody had become fascist: 'No longer is Cinisi a poor town, the current government's reforming breeze has step by step penetrated the consciousness of local people, who today are fascist from the first to the last.' The reality was that at least half of the town was illiterate, very few had baths or toilets where they lived, and 60 per cent virtually never ate any meat. The only cases of violence and lawlessness that would now be allowed were those committed by the government. So a new system of police field guards was set up, illegal connections to water supply were stopped and those in debt were cut off.

But to some extent Mafia activity continued. One of the victims was Gaspare Cucinella, an old man who ran a corner shop on the Corso, selling flour and beans. 'Binardinu' Palazzolo and his brothers had been demanding protection money but Cucinella had refused to pay. Then one day in 1937 when Cucinella was out in the countryside he saw the Palazzolos coming and knew what they meant to do, but they got the first shot in and – *ammazzarono*. They then tied Cucinella's dead body to his cart, and his donkey made its way home, delivering a dead husband to his distraught wife.

The longer the Second World War continued, the more the fascist regime began to unravel, and the Mafia to resurface. Just a few weeks after Mussolini's declaration of war in June 1940, French bombers attacked Palermo twice, an event that caused a mass exodus from the Sicilian capital. Several thousands ended up in Cinisi and the surrounding countryside, either staying with relatives, or in empty houses, barns, stables or even caves. They were not entirely safe here either, as later in the war Allied planes would regularly strafe the station and any trains running along the lines. The fascist council obviously had a responsibility to make sure any refugees were fed, but the inefficiency of both local and national administration meant that an expensive black market flourished quickly, and *Mafiosi* supported the new mayor who was trying to deal with an emergency situation.

One young thug who would lead a long and charmed life was Procopio 'Shorty' Di Maggio. He first came to people's attention when he pulled out a knife and killed someone during an argument. A few years later the town rumour mill held him responsible for the killing of a policeman –

naturally he wasn't convicted of either murder. As Gaspare Cucinella recalls, he brought the same attitude to bear in his private life: 'When Procopio Di Maggio met his future wife her father said he was against the marriage. So Don Procopio took out his gun and kneecapped him, and then told him: "Next time I'll kill you." That's how things were back then.'

Problems quickly mushroomed as the war came to a close. Authorities imposed taxes and duties on agricultural produce, part of which was allocated for public rations. Yet local landowners and wholesalers could see that if they managed to bypass the authorities they could make large profits selling food to a starving population, not just in Cinisi, but in nearby Palermo as well. The huge amount of money to be made meant it was relatively easy to bribe local officials and to be let through road blocks, otherwise these newly created criminal gangs quickly became powerful enough to shoot it out with the police if the police decided to resist them. Quick to seize on an opportunity, *Mafiosi* took over local mills that ground wheat into flour, thus effectively gaining control over bread and other food supplies at source.

Whether these gangs were run by true *Mafiosi* is unclear; in many ways it doesn't matter because even if they weren't, they acted just like them, and in any event by the 1950s a stable and widely recognised Mafia structure had emerged in the town. A clear sign of increased criminal confidence was revealed after a mayor appointed by the Allies resigned in February 1946. Soon after the new mayor took office, a grenade exploded one night outside his house, apparently a warning that the authorities shouldn't check up on the food rationing system.

A New Opposition

Just as the Mafia resurfaced in Cinisi after the end of fascism, so too did the fight against organised crime. Here and elsewhere in Sicily, for well over a century, mass opposition to the Mafia has not concentrated on polite parliamentary

politics but on local resistance, which has often been led by
Communists and Socialists.

The Communist Party opened a branch in Sicily just after
the Second World War, and it was originally run by just
two men, Stefano Venuti and Filippo Maniaci. Venuti came
from a liberal middle-class family, whereas Maniaci was
far more working class. The key moment occurred when
Venuti came back to Cinisi after the war and received two
offers, the first of which he refused. The first was from Don
Masi Impastato, who offered to find him a good job, and
the other was from Maniaci, who suggested they opened a
party branch together.

One Communist activist from nearby Terrasini remembers
what happened when the new branch opened:

> I remember the inauguration of the Communist Party
> branch in Cinisi. It was in the town square, on the left
> hand side coming up the Corso. We left Terrasini with our
> huge party banner, which used to be the pole of the Fascist
> Party banner, but I had sewn on our own flag because I
> was a tailor. We had a marvellous comrade there called
> Filippo Maniaci who gave the first speech. He began by
> saying: 'comrades, we have to fight the Mafia.' There was
> a group off to the left who started to make a noise – sadly
> at that time it was normal that meetings were disrupted
> – so Maniaci shouted at them 'You're bastards, and so is
> the man standing behind you.' The man stood behind was
> no less than Cesare Manzella.

Although Communists and Socialists sometimes just
reacted instinctively, as in this case, their strategy was
to give people hope, to show them they could keep their
self-respect and resist the Mafia and its ways. The main
platform in this strategy was demanding rights: to decent
housing, employment and – in broader terms – a society
where everybody obeyed the law.

In the first national election in 1946 the party received
just three votes, and the following year its branch suffered
a bomb attack. Venuti showed what he was made of by

bravely accusing Manzella and Masi Impastato of the crime. However, they were soon released without charge. Only a huge amount of political commitment could explain why Venuti and Maniaci didn't give in and choose an easy life. So they stuck at it: in 1948 the party's vote rose to 130, and throughout the 1950s it scored an average of around 700 votes in the town.

In 1948 a dispute erupted over the building of a road from Cinisi to Furi, which was an illustration of what was to become a vital area of Mafia money making in the 1960s: contracts awarded by public authorities. Once the contract to build the road was awarded the local Mafia demanded a rake-off for 'protection'. The company refused, and for their pains their equipment was blown up twice – after which they started paying. But it was the workers who had to pay for their employers' decision to agree to bribes: the company told them they would work an hour for free in order to finance the Mafia. The 54 workers, most of them union members, held a union meeting that was also attended by Venuti, and agreed to strike. Half an hour after Venuti left, Procopio Di Maggio arrived and told them: 'Do be careful. You can see that we can put your heads where you've got your feet. So let's try and do the right thing and just get food on the table – without contacting the union.'

The strike was called off, the Mafia had won again. To survive, people like Venuti were not only forced to be very courageous, but at times they felt obliged to act like *Mafiosi*. When Venuti heard that local Mafia leaders had decided to kill him he coolly walked into their favourite bar, and calmly said out loud:

> Here I am. These people have to know two things: firstly, if something were to happen to me or my comrades, even their pets will be shot down like dogs – and we will respect nobody, neither women nor children. Secondly, their names are already known, and when the time is right they will be passed on to those who need to know.

The fact that Venuti came from a very comfortable middle-class background, that he was a sensitive and imaginative person, an amateur poet and painter, and yet he was behaving like this, shows how living in a Mafia environment distorts normal human behaviour. In any event, every evening Venuti would walk down the same country lane to see his girlfriend, and nothing ever happened to him. The bluff worked.

Because of this climate of intimidation, Venuti and others went further by organising public meetings; it was important to destroy the sense of isolation, fear and hopelessness, to show everybody that there was opposition to the Mafia. He remembers one person who always used to listen to him: 'I recall one small boy who came to all my speeches. While everybody else of his age was running around and playing, he would listen to everything I said sitting on the kerb. When I first met him my first impression was of a boy full of enthusiasm and a huge desire for honesty and justice.'

That young boy was called Peppino Impastato.

6

The Impastatos

The Impastato family were fairly typical for Cinisi. When Felicia Bartolotta married Luigi Impastato in 1947 it was a very good deal for the groom, who had spent a couple of years 'in exile' on the island of Ustica during the fascist period, suspected of Mafia membership. Under this legal restriction people were ordered to reside in exile in another town, in an attempt to prevent them from coming into contact with the wrong sort of people.

Luigi was a short squat man with a flat nose, the son of a cattle farmer. One of his cousins was Don Masi Impastato, a local landowner and old-fashioned Mafia boss in Cinisi during the postwar period. Another relative was Nick 'Killer' Impastato, who had emigrated to the US in 1927 and was arrested as the second in command of the country's largest heroin ring in 1943. Luckily for Nick, he only served two years, but the main witness against him was unlucky in that he was murdered soon after Nick was released from jail. After a four-year legal battle, he was finally deported from Kansas City back to Italy in 1955.

That was more of an American story though. Indeed, the small minority of Italian migrants such as Nick Impastato, who turned into gangsters, has led to decades of generalised racist stereotyping of Italian-Americans, despite the fact that the vast majority didn't go down that road. But as regards Luigi Impastato and the Mafia, what really brought him in was the marriage of one of his sisters to Don Cesare Manzella.

That's not to say that Luigi Impastato ever had an important role to play: he earned his living transporting cheese and doing other odd jobs. His son Giovanni remembers that in the immediate postwar period: 'My father earned money by dealing in illegal cigarettes and wheat. He had three lorries, so he moved these things illegally to avoid paying duties and taxes on them.' In later years he was given a shop to run, and it's possible that a business with such a high cash flow was used to recycle dirty money. He was lucky to marry into a good family and inherited various plots of land.

Felicia Bartolotta was different from her husband in many respects. She had a long thin face and came from a 'good family', both in the sense that her closest relatives were not linked to the Mafia, and also because her father had a stable job working at the council; she also brought various pieces of land to the marriage. Felicia was unaware of Luigi's Mafia links: 'I didn't know what my husband was. I knew he was sent into exile – he must have done something.' Partly because she didn't know the ugly truth about his allegiances, she genuinely liked him, but 'as soon as we got married all hell broke loose'. She had become the wife of someone with a very traditional attitude towards family and marriage, a real *padre padrone*: 'He used to argue at the drop of a hat, and you never knew what he was doing or where he was going.' Gaspare Cucinella, a few years younger than Luigi, remembers him thus: 'Luigi was very uncommunicative. You could never chat with him. It was always just: "hello, how are you?" . . . "hello how are you?" . . . it never went further than that.'

Their first son, Peppino, was born in 1948, in a now-abandoned house behind the main church. He wasn't just born into the family of a low-level Mafia member, but Mafia boss and relative Don Masi Impastato lived next door, and the up-and-coming boss Procopio Di Maggio lived just behind them.

Although his mother accepted that being a woman meant she was treated as an inferior being, her desire to protect her son pushed her into conflict with her husband from the very beginning. This was the period of the notorious bandit gang led by Salvatore Giuliano, which had murdered – *ammazzarono* – 12 peasants on May Day 1947. Not only were the gang based in the nearby town of Montelepre, they also regularly killed policemen in shoot-outs, so sometimes suspected *Mafiosi* were rounded up in the next towns. Her husband knew a local policeman, and, as Felicia recounts:

> They'd told my husband there would be round-ups that night. I was terrified – whenever I saw policemen my heart used to pound. There was knocking at the door, it was the cops. Peppino was really tiny at the time. I told my husband: 'Murderer, why don't you get out? Why have you stayed home? Didn't you know they were meant to come?'

However, it was the unexpected consequences of the birth of their second son Giovanni that were, in the long term, to tear the family apart and put Cinisi on the map. Giovanni had died of encephalitis, an inflammation of the brain caused by contagious infection, so Peppino was sent to live with his maternal aunt and uncle, Fara and Matteo, who essentially raised him. Looking back on this set-up, Peppino's mother was satisfied that her son lived in a conventional family structure, in that he 'grew up in a family that had a brother, a sister and a mother. In a way his mother and father were a bit distant. But I was comfortable with this because I knew my brother would keep him on the straight and narrow . . .'

There may have been other reasons, because this was a highly unusual arrangement. In the long term this different existence – compared to the norm of a rigidly conventional family structure – may have influenced his future development. But as a boy Peppino behaved like any other, playing football on a piece of waste ground by pushing two sticks into the ground and fixing a fishing net between them. In any event, as his mother adds in a masterful piece of understatement: 'in fact he grew up different'. Giovanni, the third son who was born a couple of years later (and named after the child who had died), many years later defined his elder brother Peppino in the following terms: 'For this culture, Peppino's break with his family was a historical turning point.'

Peppino came under the influence of his uncle Matteo, who was a clerk at the council and therefore relatively well educated. He saw that Peppino had a talent for studying and he encouraged him to go further and paid for his schoolbooks. When Peppino was a teenager Matteo took him to his first meetings of the Italian Communist Party.

Peppino's rebellious spirit began to emerge when he went to high school in the nearby town of Partinico. His mother remembers the day he handed in a Latin essay:

> the teacher made a correction because according to her he'd made a mistake, but Peppino said 'There's no mistake here!' In other words they started arguing and she told him: 'You blackguard, go and sit down!' As soon as he could, he got hold of a dictionary to find out what the word meant, and all hell broke loose when he got home. My brother went and spoke with the headmaster: Peppino was in the right, he hadn't made a mistake and to top it all she had insulted him!

Meanwhile, his father only saw him occasionally, and essentially just tried to show off his first-born to his Mafia friends. To be shunted around by a distant father like some kind of trophy must have been irritating for any adolescent, but given that he was growing up outside his father's influence, the gap could only grow wider over time.

Back at the family home, Felicia Bartolotta remembers: 'My husband would tell me nothing. I had to work everything out for myself.' It wouldn't have taken much to work out why the police would often call asking to question Luigi, who habitually hid himself inside a large family chest down in the basement. Felicia started to show the first signs of being a free spirit: 'my mother had taught me about the Mafia', and made it very clear to her husband that her family would not be a Mafia family: 'so I told him – "I don't want people who are on the run staying in my house". And my husband answered – "well, what if he's a friend of mine . . .?" "I don't care, I wouldn't even care if it was my dad." I've never taken anyone in.'

The problem was that the Mafia was all around her, and in a town like Cinisi there is no wall that can be built to keep it out of sight and out of contact. Not only was Felicia living with a low-level *Mafioso*, she was closely related to the town boss, Cesare Manzella. She could maybe hold the line with her husband, but not with her brother-in-law. Despite all that happened in between, looking back many years later Felicia said this about Cesare Manzella: 'He used to come visiting and was very kind . . . I can't speak badly of him.'

One day Felicia found out that Luigi was having an affair with a neighbour and moved back in with her mother, taking Giovanni with her. But Cesare Manzella came and spoke to her, using the coded language typical of a *Mafioso*: 'Well, you know how things are.' He also went to speak to her brother Matteo, who was looking after Peppino. Afterwards Matteo advised his sister: 'Look, Felicia, move back because there's nothing else you can do.' In order to keep a lid on things and avoid any public scandal, Manzella then gave some money to the woman involved in the affair in order to keep her quiet. As Felicia says in her colourful Sicilian: 'your blood remains dirty, you're sick to your stomach'.

It was also in the day-to-day etiquette of showing respect to your relatives and friends that Felicia was unable to keep the Mafia at bay. She remembers: 'My husband and Badalamenti were like brothers.' The head of the house naturally wanted his children to meet his friends and associates, so, as their youngest child Giovanni recalls:

> My father often took me to birthday parties at the houses of *Mafiosi*. Many *Mafiosi*, including Tano Badalamenti, would come in this very house and talk with my father, all of this happened often. Badalamenti always moved about

with an entourage. He was always very correct and kind with me. The way he showed his Mafia power was through simplicity, he was very communicative even though he couldn't speak Italian very well. But through the Mafia code of communicating he was able to transmit fear very easily, he was very charismatic. He wasn't one of those show-offs who would take his gun out, he was very cool.

The problem is that the Mafia is like a spider's web; once you're caught you can't escape. People might think that just respecting social conventions means they can keep their distance from more serious entanglement. If they're very lucky things can work out that way, but although he was small fry, the head of the Impastato household was all for encouraging these connections. But in a highly dictatorial organisation like the Mafia he didn't make those decisions.

One day Manzella made sure Felicia and Giovanni went and stayed in one of his houses in the village of Contessa Entellina, where Giovanni's uncle and *Mafioso* Giuseppe 'Leadspitter' Impastato worked. Despite his nickname, those who knew Giuseppe remember him as a chubby and friendly man, but even back then, in the 1950s, Manzella had started to use the gravy train of Christian Democrat politicians and had got 'Leadspitter' a job as a field guard on the land of local MP Antonio Pecoraro.

Through their control over the political system, and the public sector economy, Christian Democrats were able to manage and allocate precious resources, such as jobs. The Mafia often acted as a filter in this system: forwarding requests upwards to politicians and receiving favours in return. The key link between the politicians and *Mafiosi* was the Mafia's ability to deliver votes, although sometimes the two roles could be combined in just one person.

The most notorious example from this period was Giuseppe Genco Russo, the head of the Mafia after the death of Don Calogero Vizzini in 1954. Genco Russo had first come to the authorities' attention as far back as 1927, when the Caltanissetta police chief had written that Genco Russo's wealth had been gained 'with profits from crime and the Mafia'; he had also taken part in the Hotel Delle Palme summit in Palermo in 1957. Genco Russo had briefly been secretary of the Christian Democrat branch in his hometown, and when he stood as a councillor in Mussomeli in October 1960 a row broke out during an election debate on television. The party provincial secretary immediately told the press, 'Mr Genco Russo is just like anyone else, and as such has the right to be a Christian Democrat candidate in Mussomeli.' Even party leader Aldo Moro defended his candidature, so not surprisingly he was elected.

To come back to Cinisi, why was Cesare Manzella being so generous by inviting the Impastatos to stay in his country house? The reason emerged soon after, when a double murder took place in the town – *ammazzarono*; he wanted to make sure Felicia and her son were not around. On one hand Felicia must have appreciated Manzella's gesture, but on the other her blood must have run cold when she thought about how deeply she was compromised. She often went and stayed at his house during the holidays, but again couldn't fail to notice what was happening: 'Sometimes I saw certain people. I once met Luciano Leggio. I had nothing to do with him but I understood what was going on. He slept there, and then in the morning they took him somewhere else.'

Known as the 'Scarlet Pimpernel' for his long periods on the run, Leggio was far from being the romantic figure his nickname suggests. His rapid rise within the organisation began when, as a 23-year-old, he murdered a Socialist trade unionist named Placido Rizzotto in his hometown of Corleone back in 1948. By the late 1950s he had gained control of the Corleone clan, which has dominated the Mafia since the late 1970s, and tutored the man who remained boss until his capture in April 2006 – Bernardo 'the Tractor' Provenzano. At the time Felicia met him, she would have known that Leggio was one of the main leaders of the Mafia, and was on the run from the police when he stayed in the same house as her.

Whether she liked it or not, Felicia was in deep. She faced a choice: if she told the police where to find one of the country's most wanted fugitives, she would have had to go into hiding in order to stay alive, along with her children and husband, yet at that time the police did not have anything approaching a witness protection programme. And even if they did, Manzella would have killed her other relatives, so if she had decided to be an honest citizen it would have meant her death and that of her immediate family, or many of her close relatives. In situations like this *Mafiosi* can see that people have chosen to turn a blind eye to their activities. But what drags people in even deeper is the awareness of having become an accessory to serious crimes by not reporting them. Regardless of your own personal views, your safety becomes linked to that of Mafia leaders.

While all this was going on their eldest child, Peppino, was developing in a completely independent way. His mother remembers him going to hear the Communist activist Stefano Venuti speak: 'He used to listen to all his speeches. He'd sit on the kerb with his hands like this; he was against the Christian Democrats. Me and Venuti knew each other, so I said to him: "Mr Venuti, would you do me a favour? Would you get my boy to stop this?" "Why should he, he's an intelligent boy."'

Although his mother might have been understanding, Peppino's father was not. One day Peppino came home and told his father he'd passed his exams: 'My uncle has bought me a raincoat and a bag to carry my books. What are you going to give me?' Sometimes Peppino could be a bit too pushy and sarcastic with his father, failing to show the respect that was normal for the time. So his father answered coldly: 'What am I going to give you? Nothing. When you decide to leave the Communist Party is when I'll buy you something.' Given that his attitude tended to create confrontation, at a very young age Peppino was forced to make a choice between developing his own ideas, or submitting to tradition and having a normal family life.

A key turning point came when his uncle Don Cesare Manzella was killed by a car bomb in the First Mafia War. Shocked, Peppino told his mother, 'these people really are criminals'. She remembered, 'That's when it all started. He started talking about bullying, about injustice.' Although aged just 15, Peppino made a conscious decision: 'if this is what the Mafia is, then I'm going to oppose it'. If he had been living under the same roof as his Mafia father it would have been unlikely that he thought in this way, and what he went on to do was simply unheard of at the time. For a small sleepy town such as Cinisi, Peppino's actions were going to be truly shocking.

'The Mafia – A Mountain of Shit'

Contrary to some stereotypes, Peppino was a left-wing activist with emotions. Indeed, perhaps this brief poem he wrote expresses the self-denial that is inevitable in what was virtually full-time political activity:

> Men look at the sky
> And are amazed,
> They look at the earth
> And they feel compassion
> But oddly,
> They do not notice themselves.

In the following quotation he expresses in more formal language what happened to him as a teenager:

> I got involved in politics way back in November '65 on a purely emotional basis, in other words it began from my need to react against the unbearable situation within my family. My father, head of a little clan and member of a bigger clan, had since my birth tried to impose on me his choices and behavioural patterns – with the ideological connotations typical of a late peasant and pre-industrial society. All he managed to do was to cut off all emotional communication . . . I got involved with the Italian Socialist Party for Workers' Unity with all the anger and desperation of somebody who was simultaneously trying to destroy everything and find protection. We set up a strong youth

group, created a newspaper and a new way of thinking, ended up in court and in all the newspapers.

These were the days before the Internet – indeed, many local people still had no television – so the method Peppino and his friends used to spread their views was a newspaper, *L'Idea Socialista* (*Socialist Idea*).

By today's standards the contents of this small newspaper might seem tame, but reaction in the town showed that it was viewed as revolutionary. The first taboo subject they broached was women's rights and sex. Italy was still backward in this field; for example, the penal code sanctioned harsher punishments for women than for men in cases of adultery, and there was a huge debate in Sicily in 1965 when a woman who had been raped refused to marry her attacker. The first major article in the paper supporting local women's criticism of male chauvinism appeared in March 1967 and, significantly, was written by a man. A few months later the same writer and Peppino returned to the subject, stating:

> In Cinisi the majority of young women respond to their first sexual instincts in one way: by suppressing or denying them, with consequences that are easy to imagine . . . the fear of gossiping leads them to create unstable relationships with boys (with whom they obviously meet in secret), to whom they give complete attention, something which becomes unhealthy in a suffocating environment of repressed sexuality.
>
> They normally meet 'on the quiet' due to understandable 'fears', and rather than feeling satisfied they can feel embittered and may suffer some kind of mental disturbance.

Such discussion meant coming into conflict with the self-appointed guardian of public morals, the Church. Another early editorial emphasised that the paper was aiming at a new generation of young people: 'Perhaps these young people don't go to church, but they have a strong moral sense that is no longer held back by prejudiced dogma. This is an expression of a consciousness that sees the evils of the world and is upset by them, and tries to bring some relief to the victims.'

The issues the *Socialist Idea* raised were also tangible ones. For example, in one article it attacked both the fact that apart from two well-lit streets: 'the rest of the town seems illuminated by candlelight', and that the town only had water for five hours a day. They accused the mayor of not insisting that a councillor from the same party, upon whose private land there was a large fresh water well, agree to supply the town with water at an acceptable rate.

Stefano Venuti, the best-known Communist activist in town, also contributed to the paper, openly denouncing corruption following local elections:

> This occurs in various ways – the outright buying of votes (a packet of pasta, 1 to 10,000 lire, a promise of a job, a favour, etc). And here a 'favour' can mean anything: a prisoner who will be released from jail, a patient who will not pay hospital fees, a consumer who will not pay water rates or council tax, or somebody else who will get planning permission or a licence to trade.

But Peppino and his friends were also breaking from the Communist Party, the only organisation that had managed to be some kind of opposition to corrupt local politicians and the Mafia. Although the Communist Party is not named in the following editorial it is clear that this is the organisation the writer has in mind. This stress on practical action is important to mention again, because such a strategy was to shake the town over the next ten years:

> if you look back you realise that in Cinisi the working class and the socialist tradition cannot boast of class struggle, nor popular demands or protests. This has undoubtedly contributed to the emergence of a significant gap between workers and peasants and the political parties that represent them. Furthermore, it has stunted the growth

of a broad working class which is aware of its purpose, merits and strength.

In essence, over this two-year period Peppino and others were becoming revolutionaries, rejecting the politics of the Socialist and Communist Parties, all of which had been tried and tested, but had failed to really change things. There had been great anticipation in 1963 when the Socialists had joined a national government after 16 years in opposition, but their enthusiasm for reform was quickly blocked and blunted by the Christian Democrats. The main hope of the Communist Party was to win a majority in parliament and form a government – something distinctly unlikely in the medium and long term, given the Cold War politics that dominated Italy. Local Communist activists such as Venuti might have influenced Peppino, but often the hands of these individuals were tied by regional and national leaders, and they were forced into alliances with dodgy Christian Democrats.

On an international scale, young people such as Peppino had new models too, such as the Cuban and Vietnam national liberation struggles, or looked to individuals like Che Guevara, and genuinely believed that Mao's China was a shining example of a new socialism. Local Communists tried to compete: when Che Guevara was killed in Bolivia the local branch produced a booklet, but after the single page on Che there were eight pages on the Russian revolution of 1917, often in the form of a series of events listed chronologically and ending in a statement by the party's general secretary – hardly the sort of stuff to capture the imagination of young people.

The second biggest taboo that Peppino and others broke was to talk about the Mafia. This is how his mother Felicia found out what her 17-year-old son was doing:

> I knew nothing about it because I was staying in the countryside. I slept downstairs, and Peppino and my brother upstairs. Peppino would be writing away, and from time to time my brother would have a look at what

he was reading. Then he came downstairs – 'Felicia'. 'What
is it?' 'Have you seen that Peppino is coming out against
the Mafia?' And I said: 'Oh my God, what am I going to do
about my husband?' He was a touch aggressive, and used
to hit us. Peppino didn't get hit a lot because he wasn't
home that much, but Giovanni copped quite a bit. I used
to jump in the middle and got hit a few times as well.

Giovanni says his father never hit him. It is possible he
has genuinely forgotten, or is embarrassed by the memory
– or that his mother was exaggerating. Regardless of the
specific level of violence within the Impastato family, these
are very much the attitudes and dynamics within a Mafia
family, and it is through repeated treatment of this kind
that future generations of *Mafiosi* are shaped.

Even though Peppino probably got off lightly compared
to his brother, he also had other problems to worry about.
The Christian Democrat mayor (also magistrate and cousin
of Gaetano Badalamenti), Domenico Pellerito, reported the
content of the *Socialist Idea* to the police. Within five days
of its first appearance on newsagents' shelves the small
group of young editors were called into the police station
to explain themselves. The police then launched an official
investigation, and later questioned the youths individually.
They reached the conclusion that it was an illegal publication
because it had been published secretly, and a magistrate
gave them a suspended sentence. The editors appealed,
and the legal dance continued.

Why did the mayor react so quickly, and the authorities
so harshly? Hard as it is to believe, the answer is sport. The
paper criticised the lack of facilities in the town in an article
which contained the following sentence: 'Perhaps Cinisi's
first citizen is completely unaware of the meaning of the
word sport, and the lack of interest of council officials is
obvious – this is a slap in the face for all sports enthusiasts
in town.' The fact this harmless article could have created
such a bizarre response shows there was no real political
discussion in town; the Communist opposition had failed
to stir things up. Everybody knew their place. Nobody criticised the local establishment.

One of the most important outcomes was that the legal to-ings and fro-ings meant the paper couldn't be published for nearly a year. It is highly likely that the 'offending article' was not the real reason for the clampdown but was merely a pretext. Given that the paper dealt with corruption, emigration and sexual repression – in anyone's book far more important issues than sport – the authorities were probably just looking for an excuse. Yet once it started to be published again in early 1966 the paper began attacking in even more aggressive tones the politicians who had attempted to close it down.

One notorious article written by Peppino exploded like a bomb through the town. It was entitled: 'The Mafia – A Mountain of Shit'. His mother went to visit the parents of all the other boys involved in the paper and asked them to persuade their children to stop what they were doing. She was stunned to discover that these parents supported their actions. Although her primary concern was to protect her own son, the fact that other parents were behind the paper must have in some way forced her to realise Peppino was in the right.

All editors suffered harassment because of the paper's content, but Peppino more than most. One day soon after the publication of the 'Mountain of Shit' article the Impastatos heard a knock on the door of their house on the Corso, it was the old Mafia patriarch Don Masi Impastato. Luigi went outside to talk to him, and the old don told Peppino's father, 'If that was my son, I'd dig a grave and bury him in it.' Felicia was listening behind the blinds, and at that point could not contain her protective instincts and burst out to shout at him, 'you're skating on very thin ice if you carry on making threats like that'.

'Leadspitter' Impastato, Peppino's uncle, told Luigi that this kind of thing could not happen in a Mafia family. These were just the first two angry responses from a pair of *Mafiosi*. Such comments were in all likelihood just opinions and nothing more, however, over the next few years Peppino's behaviour meant that angry comments became calculated threats.

Peppino had moved back home a year or two earlier to live with his parents when he was about 18, because one of the relatives he had been living with had died and another had got married. But now his father had lost face, not only with the town at large but also with his Mafia friends in particular. So he kicked him out, and Peppino went back to live with his aunt and uncle.

Luigi Impastato must have remembered something Cesare Manzella had said to him a few years earlier: 'But what kind of family have you got involved in, what are you playing at?' For a father, not being able to control his family is a humiliating sign of weakness. Although Luigi would never admit it, he had lost the battle to control his son, and his behaviour only increased Peppino's determination to rebel against his father's values. When Luigi got angry he'd tell his wife: 'Leave, and take your sons with you.' This only entrenched divisions, as Peppino's uncle Matteo would come to visit Felicia rather than her husband.

Life in the Impastato household became like a pressure cooker, as Giovanni recalls:

> My mother was the wife of a *Mafioso* and the mother of a left-wing activist who fought against the Mafia. She was in a very difficult situation because she was right in the middle. She didn't want me to go down the same road as Peppino . . . she treated me normally, but she was always more worried about Peppino because he was in far more danger. It wasn't that she didn't care about me or didn't love me, she was just very worried about what could happen to Peppino. It's as if this family has lived a kind of Greek tragedy, with my mother forever at a crossroads. Because she was a Christian the family was sacred, and you had to respect your husband.

Felicia was born during the First World War, and still belonged to that time and culture. This meant that she had to be a wife to her husband and a mother to her children, servicing all of them materially and emotionally, yet she knew she couldn't play either of these roles adequately.

Peppino's horizons, meanwhile, started to broaden. He got involved with the civil rights activist Danilo Dolci in the nearby town of Partinico, where he went to secondary school. He went on a five-day 'March of Protest and Hope' through the Sicilian countryside, ending in Palermo. He learned perhaps for the first time that the Mafia exists because of a lack of economic development and real alternatives, one very concrete example being the shortage of water caused by the government refusing to build dams to create reservoirs – and all the while the Mafia controlled precious fresh water wells. One of the other issues was the Vietnam War, the Iraq of Peppino's generation. The final speech of the march was given by Vo Van Ai, a leader of the Vietnamese resistance, whose words were published by the *Socialist Idea*:

> For a solution to be created, it is necessary that peoples throughout the world put pressure on their governments so that they unanimously demand:
>
> 1) An immediate end to all American bombing in Vietnam.
> 2) An end to America's support of the Ky government in South Vietnam.
> 3) The creation of a civilian government in the South elected by the people, free of all foreign interference, able to work effectively for peace by negotiating an end to hostilities and moving towards reunification.

The Vietnam War was on news bulletins daily around the world, and many young people were starting to oppose American involvement. By publishing this article, and many others, the *Socialist Idea* began to draw in its young readers.

Yet the paper was not dealing only with politics in the abstract, or events occurring half a world away. It carried on attacking the corruption of local politicians, who continued to demand that action be taken against it; the new mayor, a Social Democrat, had once again called on the police to take action. The party that had sponsored the paper, meanwhile, withdrew its support, and the police were now telling the editors – now just Peppino and one other – that the paper had to be closed down. It did close, yet Peppino had other ideas he wanted to try out.

7

Welcome to Mafiopoli

The police finally caught sight of Gaetano Badalamenti at Palermo Airport on 26 July 1969, getting off a flight from Rome. They'd lost trace of him since he disappeared back in 1963 to avoid both an arrest warrant, and the people who wanted to kill him in the First Mafia War.

It was fitting that he should be resurfacing at the airport, in many ways it was a monument to his power. It was controversial when it opened in 1960 because it stood next to a mountain, and was therefore liable to suffer from unpredictable winds and air turbulence. So why was it ever built in the first place? One answer is that Badalamenti owned much of the land, land that had to be bought at high prices in order to develop it. The way in which *Mafiosi* often used to buy land also reveals their powers of intimidation, generally expressed indirectly. Nino Mannino, former mayor of Carini, a town on the other side of Mount Pecoraro, outlines a classic method: 'Let's say a *Mafioso* is interested in buying a piece of land. He gets a message to the current owner along the lines of: "It would be a shame to sell this without telling so-and-so." This is a coded message to tell the owner that a *Mafioso* wants to buy it.' And naturally, the owner doesn't want to offend the local Mafia boss by not offering the land to him first. Badalamenti and other Mafia leaders would also gain further from the building of the airport, as they had a controlling influence over all of the cement and earth-moving companies that would be needed for the building work.

Furthermore, if Badalamenti could control who got jobs at the airport he could kill two birds with one stone. First, by strategically placing his men he could facilitate the international drug smuggling he had been involved in for many years. And in fact, sometimes passengers' luggage did not pass through the terminal and all its checks, but was moved to and from the aircraft by trusted airport drivers. The second advantage, which represents a key social change, was that he could create consensus and support by finding scarce jobs for desperate local people.

What Badalamenti was grappling with was the fact that the whole of southern Italy was changing, from a backward agricultural society to a modern urban society. And most of this change was being managed by public authorities. So the other vital factor in the siting of Palermo's new airport in Badalamenti's back yard was that it fell within the boundaries of Cinisi city council. To some people, it looked like a gold mine.

When the proposal to build an airport first became public, the mayor of Cinisi, Antonino Orlando, told local people in a speech: 'you don't understand, the airport will make us rich – they'll pay for the land in gold'. Holding out the palms of his hands, he continued: 'here's the land and here's the gold'. In a limited sense, he was true to his word. Those who were already in the know had bought up some of these areas, only to sell them on later at ten or twenty times the original price. For local councillors all this meant gaining access to large amounts of public money. Those who profited were the architects, the consultants, the political and military committees responsible for approving various plans – and of course the Mafia. And remember that under Italian law it is legal to propose, or work on, an existing project in the morning as a consultant or architect, and in the evening to vote projects through as a councillor.

Leaving aside such practices, equally worrying was the overlooking of safety issues. When the council's plans went up to regional government, former pilots warned that the winds in that area and the close proximity to the sea and mountains made any such decision pure madness. Regional government therefore asked national government to hold a commission of inquiry. A group of air force generals then held one meeting that lasted less than two hours and decided that the airport was safe after all.

It was a huge building project, which would take three years to complete. One runway would be 3.6 kilometres long and 65 metres wide, whereas the other would be 2.7 kilometres by 45 metres. This meant a massive amount of earth moving and concrete. A company named SAB won most of the contracts because its tender was 29 per cent lower than others. But how could they do the work so much cheaper than other firms? A company controlled or influenced by the Mafia can make most of its employees work illegally – so they can pay them below the minimum wage, and also avoid paying tax and national insurance. Given that the wage bill is normally far higher than the cost of machinery and raw material, a Mafia company can still make a large profit even though it has tendered for the contract at a far lower level than its rivals.

There is another trick the Mafia can use, just in case they can't drive down wages and fiddle the books: raise the cost of the project. The original plans for developing the site, strangely, didn't include a geological survey. Then, when work started, huge subterranean caverns were 'discovered', which obviously entailed much more work and higher costs than were originally planned.

The building of the airport meant the economy started to change, the new jobs that were being created were no longer related to agriculture. Construction work was managed by Mafia-controlled contractors, so for the first time *Mafiosi* became employers in an area of high unemployment. Piero Impastato, a distant relative of Peppino, remembers when as a child he used to visit 'the patriarch of Cinisi' with his family:

> When my family went to visit Don Masi Impastato they generally used to chat and play cards. After a while, I noticed Don Masi was always surrounded by young people and I thought: 'What the fuck are these young guys doing here? They're talking to an old man!' Afterwards I worked it out: given that in our area there's always been a lot of unemployment, you either emigrate, get someone to put a word in for you somewhere in the public sector, or you become part of the Mafia. There really is no other escape route. So these people were turning up to ask him to put a word in somewhere.

Work on the airport was completed on time, and the first flight landed from Rome on the evening of 1 January 1960. Interestingly enough, at a press conference the captain said: 'We didn't know there was a mountain so close', and was overheard talking to his co-pilot about a 'crazy wind'. Three weeks later a flight from Naples suffered terrible air turbulence during its approach and the captain refused to land, flying to another airport.

Maybe the airport needed a third runway which ran in a different direction? Why not? It would mean another round of huge public sector contracts. This wasn't such a mad idea – a few miles away in Palermo all manner of tricks were being pulled in the name of progress and economic development.

The 'Sack of Palermo'

Until his murder in 1992, Salvo Lima had enjoyed forty very successful years in Sicilian politics. A tall distinguished-looking man with wavy white hair, the great enigma was that in all this time he probably made less than a dozen public speeches – yet he always received more votes than any other Christian Democrat politician in Sicily.

He became mayor of Palermo for the first time in 1958, aged just 30, holding office continuously until 1963, and again in 1965 to 1966. In 1968 he stood for parliament, made no campaign speeches, but received a massive 80,000 first-preference votes. After being re-elected several times, he stood for the European parliament in 1979. Yet, just three years earlier, the Italian parliament's permanent Anti-Mafia Commission had released a mammoth report into the Mafia, the result of ten years' research, which saw Lima's name mentioned 149 times. But such 'guilt by association' did nothing to slow Lima's career; if anything the opposite happened. In 1983 two finance police reports named him as being involved in arms trafficking to members of the Mafia, yet the following year he was re-elected with an avalanche of 246,000 preference votes.

Lima's charmed career is a warning against the simplistic arguments that the Mafia can be defeated by electing honest politicians. The majority of people voting for Lima probably presumed he was a *Mafioso*, and voted for him because they thought that both he and the Mafia could do something for them. The way politics can work in Sicily is that being linked to the Mafia doesn't necessarily mean people won't vote for you – it often means they will – in the hope of personal gain rather than out of fear.

Lima's most notorious contribution to Mafia power coincided with his term of office as mayor of the Sicilian capital, a period known as 'the sack of Palermo' due to the destruction of much of the city's architectural heritage and its replacement with ugly blocks of flats. Lima was operating in a situation where there was a huge demand for houses, Sicilians were leaving an unproductive countryside and looking for better-paid public sector and service jobs in Palermo. People – including the Mafia – were following the money.

The trick was how to award huge building contracts to your friends, who obviously couldn't actually appear to be in control of the contracts because of their criminal reputation. So, of the total of 4,205 building licences granted by Palermo council from 1959 to 1963, an incredible 80 per cent went to just five people. These individuals were later described in an official report as being: 'retired persons, of modest means, none with any experience in the building trade, and who, evidently, simply lent their names to the real builders'.

They were *prestanomi*, literally 'name lenders'. Indeed one of these pensioners later got a job as the doorkeeper of one of the blocks of flats he was supposed to have built. It was relatively easy for the many brand-new building companies to obtain credit from banks, generally they found a friendly face at those newly created banks that were being founded by the most forward-looking *Mafiosi*.

Because of all the dirty tricks and creative accounting, costs and profits were inflated. Around this period the budget for street maintenance in Palermo was 4.4 billion lire, yet in a similar-sized city, Bologna, it was 500 million – Palermo cost nine times more. It was the same for sewer and drain maintenance: 6 billion in Palermo against 200 million in Bologna – 30 times higher. Not only were consumers paying way over the odds, but the centre of Palermo was ruined. One example was Villa Deliella, a building protected due to its 'significant artistic value'. On 29 November 1959 Prince Lanza di Scalea applied to demolish it, permission was granted by the council immediately, and that night the bulldozers moved in and destroyed it.

Mafiopoli

But what had Gaetano Badalamenti been up to for the last six years? Even today, nobody knows for certain.

One thing that is sure is that he was developing his drugs trade with the US. In 1968 Italian police had charged two Italian Americans linked to Badalamenti with running a heroin distribution ring out of a pizzeria in Himroad Street, New York. Three years later an even bigger network was unearthed. The basic mechanism was Roma Foods, which distributed food to over 650 restaurants and pizzerias. Another was the Piancone Pizza Palaces chain, all owned by two of Badalamenti's nephews. It was in a New Jersey Pizza Palace that the biggest heroin seizure so far ever discovered was made by police – 86 kilos sent by Badalamenti.

Wherever he was, Badalamenti definitely knew about the development of the new airport, as well as the nearby 'sack of Palermo'. It is equally certain that somebody of his criminal stature would have been wheeling and dealing with important people. What's also sure is that at some stage Badalamenti became friends with the Salvo cousins, Nino and Ignazio, often described as the 'financial lungs' of the Christian Democrat Party. One of the Mafia's top supergrasses, Antonino Calderone, described the Salvos very differently: 'The Salvo cousins were the richest men in Italy and they were both men of honour. They were in a position to dictate things to ministers . . . The Salvos were introduced to me by Gaetano Badalamenti, who was both proud and jealous of his friendship.'

Under Italian law Sicily is defined as a 'special region', and has many central powers devolved locally, one of them being tax collection. Whereas in the rest of Italy tax collectors like the Salvo cousins cost the state an average of 3.3 per cent of the revenue collected, in Sicily the Salvos got away with keeping 10 per cent of the money they had amassed. They were also allowed to hold on to the actual revenue for inordinately long periods, thus effectively enjoying huge interest-free loans.

This is how they were able to become leading landowners, hotel operators, wine producers and real estate developers in Sicily. They were active within the party, and in all likelihood gave certain Christian Democrat leaders large private donations. The Salvos were also able to deliver a significant number of votes to party candidates in their home town. And the party gave things in return. One of the most notorious examples was the La Zagarella hotel just outside Palermo. At 1970s prices, it cost $15 million to build, but the Salvos put up just $600,000 of their own money. The rest came from public funds, controlled by the Christian Democrats. Fittingly, this was the hotel where the dominant party in government and their associates held their luxury receptions and weddings. It was also where they staged their big political meetings, at which they would invite seven-times Prime Minister Giulio Andreotti. For slightly more intimate parties, they kept a 26-metre yacht moored in Palermo harbour, aboard which were paintings by Van Gogh and Matisse.

Then there was the huge estate of thousands of acres near the town of Gela, and according to a supergrass:

> They transformed it without spending a penny of their own money. They got loans from banks, then they did the paperwork to exploit that EU law, and got the money back they had been loaned . . . Just imagine, they diverted a river and got it to pass through this big wine grove, creating six or seven small artificial lakes. Then they installed some huge pumps which irrigated the entire estate with water from the lakes. And these lakes were no joke: Nino drove me around them in a jeep and boasted that the whole operation was the apple of his eye. And he hadn't paid a thing.

Back in the early 1960s police reports were already describing the Salvo cousins as *Mafiosi* who were sons of *Mafiosi*, but they had reached such a level of wealth, power and respectability that they had become untouchable.

Apart from drug running, for people such as Badalamenti this is where the big money could be made – getting contracts and grants from public funds. This meant rubbing shoulders with the great and the good. After all, rich people who are corrupt need someone important to recycle or look after their money. In this period most top *Mafiosi* had their companies registered at the offices of Giuseppe Mandalari, who had been a parliamentary candidate for the fascist MSI party in 1972.

The other great institution and power broker in Italian society was the Church. The supergrass Antonino Calderone recalls that at the end of the 1960s Badalamenti invited him to lunch in Cinisi. The reason was to ask whether he could hide Luciano Leggio, but as he put the question a priest walked in, and Badalamenti immediately introduced him to the others as a 'man of honour', a *Mafioso*. This was Agostino Coppola, parish priest of Carini, a town on the other side of Mount Pecoraro, and cousin of top US mobster Frank 'Three Fingers' Coppola.

Agostino Coppola had his uses, such as christening children and performing wedding services for notorious gangsters on the run, such as Totò Riina's marriage in 1974 – a few years later Riina became leader of the Mafia, a position he held until his arrest in January 1993. But Coppola also had a more earthly importance, such as acting as a go-between and negotiator; on more than one occasion such a respected member of the community picked up a ransom payment during a Mafia kidnap. The fact that he was seen more than once at Mafia summits in Milan showed that he was far more than just a convenient cover or courier – he was a senior and active Mafia member. On the other side of Mount Pecoraro, the Church was equally compromised, as one anti-Mafia activist comments: 'I used to see the archbishop of Cinisi arm in arm with Giuseppe Finazzo', one of Badalamenti's most trusted lieutenants. There was a rumour in Cinisi that this priest allowed Luciano Leggio to hide out in his church. In any event, it is hard not to disagree with the following comment: 'As for taking care of people's souls, the Mafia here in Cinisi have always been very good!'

But where had Badalamenti been hiding for the last six years? Again, nobody knows for sure. But in all likelihood he was often 'hiding' at home, in Cinisi.

One of the young men in Cinisi who was starting to rebel against his Mafia background remembered that during this time: 'Very often I used to see these police – and this was something that annoyed me intensely – going off to have a coffee with *Mafiosi*. Sometimes people might say "what does that prove?", but to me and lots of other people it was obvious what going to the bar with *Mafiosi* meant, everyone knew they were *Mafiosi*.' He was right. In a Mafia-ridden town, for a policeman to go to a bar with a *Mafioso* means the same thing as handing over the keys to the jail. The important thing about it was that everybody saw it happening and understood what it meant – that these people were friends, they would help each other out. A well-known opponent of the Mafia remembers: 'The police never had any problems with the *Mafiosi*, they had problems with us! So people used to see who the authorities dealt with and drew their own conclusions.' All these messages came over clearer than front-page headlines in a newspaper, because everybody in town followed the local gossip. Badalamenti too once recalled a senior local officer thus: 'when somebody wanted to have a coffee . . . he wanted to have a coffee. But only he would pay, he wouldn't let anyone else pay.' In always paying, the policeman wanted everyone to know that he intended to cultivate this relationship – for whatever reason.

It is not surprising then, that according to another Mafia supergrass, it was widely known that Badalamenti and his gang: 'had the police stations of Cinisi and Terrasini in their pocket'. So when Badalamenti was facing an arrest warrant: 'sometimes he went on the run in Cinisi, particularly in the summer. It was quiet there, nobody went looking for him.' Obscenity piles upon obscenity: through much of the 1960s police issued Badalamenti, of all people, with a gun licence.

In a typically indirect manner, the Mafia would send messages to keen young officers who arrived in the town. Pino Manzella recalls:

> I always remember that back then, whenever a new police superintendent arrived, soon afterwards there was a bank robbery. The superintendent then somehow understood he had to behave in a certain way, and after that there were no more bank robberies, break-ins, etc etc. The bank robbery was a message which said: 'unless you mind your own business, and allow us to mind ours, then there will be a lot more bank robberies.' Sometimes a housebreaker would disappear. Rather than taking him to the police they would kill him and burn his car. So back then nothing ever happened, you could leave your door unlocked at night, nothing would happen. Things were totally calm here, but this was due more to the Mafia than the police . . .

Such an arrangement helped the police, as it contributed to keeping the overall crime rate down, and for the Mafia it meant less patrols and investigations – and therefore better conditions to run their illegal businesses.

Indeed, Salvatore Maltese, a long-term fascist councillor, recalled that other traditional 'pillars of the community' had a very small role to play: 'There was a time here when lawyers had no work at all. This was because all disputes were settled by *Mafiosi*. Whenever there was a dispute over land boundaries, or problems between a man and a woman, or animals that had been stolen, people turned to them.' But sometimes even Don Tano was unlucky enough to be arrested, although he was rarely charged and never convicted of a serious crime until the mid-1980s. Nevertheless, he would need inside help when he was in the Ucciardone, Palermo's main jail – and here things become even more surprising.

Back in the mid-1950s, Christian Democrat politicians such as Salvo Lima, following national party policy, launched big campaigns of 'moralisation' and 'renewal' within the party. One of these 'renewers' was a young doctor named Francesco Barbaccia, who when he first stood for parliament was completely unknown, gave no speeches, yet received the highest vote of all Christian Democrat candidates in Sicily. For several years he continued in the same vein, writing no articles and giving no speeches. What he got in exchange from Lima's council for such commitment were favourable decisions on his building investments, and his brother was appointed leader of the council's tourism committee.

One thing Barbaccia did bother to do was write a letter supporting the passport application of one of the most powerful Mafia killers, Tommaso Buscetta, describing him as 'a person who interests me a great deal'. Years later, as a supergrass, Buscetta revealed what the interest was – Buscetta would deliver thousands of votes to Barbaccia and help get him elected. But maybe Barbaccia's heart wasn't really in making money, or in helping Mafia killers, after all, he was a doctor. As well as being an MP for a decade, he also worked in Palermo prison from 1964 to 1993. Several supergrasses have confirmed that he was a *Mafioso*, probably part of Badalamenti's clan, and would convey messages to and from prison inmates.

Not for nothing did Felicia, mother of the two Impastato brothers, once say: 'In Cinisi Don Tano protected people who minded their own business, he helped people across the board, if they needed to go into hospital . . .' – or any other favours. Councillor Maltese recounts one of many emblematic episodes:

> There was a retired police officer who wanted to place a water butt on the pavement outside the front of his house to collect water. He applied to the council but they turned him down. But he knew that Badalamenti had one outside his house, which had been authorised by the council. So he went to Badalamenti and said: 'I know that for you I'm just a filthy cop, but how come they gave you permission and not me?' 'Don't worry about it,' he told him, 'I'll sort it out.' Then he phoned the council, which immediately granted permission – that's the kind of atmosphere we lived in back then.

Badalamenti and the authorities were two sides of the same coin. As Giovanni Impastato once testified to the Anti-Mafia Commission:

> It seems that Badalamenti was well-liked by the police as he was calm, reliable and always liked a chat. It almost felt like he was doing them a favour in that nothing ever happened in Cinisi, it was a quiet little town. If anything, we were subversives who made nuisances of ourselves. This was what the police thought. When I chanced to speak to one of them – something which didn't happen often because I didn't really trust them – I realised that it was a widely held belief that Tano Badalamenti was a gentleman and it was us who were the trouble-makers . . . I often used to see them walking arm in arm with Tano Badalamenti and his henchmen.

Giovanni's brother Peppino once coined a name that brought all these changes together – the fact that Sicily was becoming both urbanised and dominated by the Mafia. Whether it was Cinisi or Palermo, for many people the idea they were living in a 'Mafiopoli' wasn't far wrong.

8

Bulldozers, Builders and Brothers

After the closure of the *Socialist Idea*, the next activity that was to worry the legal and illegal establishment of Cinisi was the setting up of the 'Che Club', named after Che Guevara, the Argentinian revolutionary murdered by the CIA in the Bolivian jungle in 1967. Once again, it was Peppino Impastato who played a central role.

A young girl at the time, Felicetta Vitale remembers the first time she saw Peppino:

> My parents ran the *Bar Roma* on the *Corso* – nowadays my brother runs it. In fact I first met Peppino in that bar, when I was a little girl. Peppino's group used our bar regularly, it was the 'students' bar'. He used to come in with his friends and they'd be discussing things – but he was *unreachable*. I really admired him because I could see he was a real leader. He was small in height, shorter than Giovanni.

As is often the case, in order to become a leader, individuals often develop an intense, moody, almost withdrawn personality, and to a large extent this was what Peppino was like.

In any event, once the decision was made to set up the Che Club, Peppino found a room owned by his family that could be used as a meeting place. Apart from the inevitable Che Guevara, one activist recalls that: 'On the walls of our office there were posters of Marx, Engels, Stalin, Lenin and Mao, and our future was mapped out by Lin Piao – go further to the left.' It may seem strange today, but back then the myth of Mao Zedong and other Chinese leaders was very strong; during the 1968 election it was discovered that in Cinisi 13 ballot papers had been spoiled by people sticking on a photo of the Chinese leader. Three hundred copies of Mao's *Little Red Book* were distributed in Cinisi alone, and were often waved about during demonstrations. Giuseppe Nobile remembers what getting involved in a Maoist group meant in Partinico, the first town you encounter moving inland from Cinisi:

> I remember seeing them in the square of Partinico in the summer of 1969 – including some friends from high school – with their flags and red handkerchiefs, trying to make some headway with local people. They used the language of the Cultural Revolution in China, and their models were the Red Guards. They tried to recruit local people on the spot – today the equivalent would be Jehovah's Witnesses – most of the membership were young fanatical people. They were very naïve: they would talk to these old peasants about revolution being the birth of a new humanity. Their analysis was that Italy was ripe for revolution, so you needed a programme for a revolutionary government.
>
> Our political activity wasn't so much against the Christian Democrats, but against the whole system. This was our great weakness: we were long-sighted, we never brought into focus what was close to us. For us politics was an ideological choice you made, a view of the world – we weren't interested in who individually ran the system or who got the biggest vote at elections. For us it was

logical to go beyond all this: we never knew exactly when or how, but at some point in the future people would agree with us and we would find ourselves in power. We were strongly influenced by Third World struggles – where the countryside surrounded the cities.

Although much of Maoist thought and practice was childishly and irrelevantly radical, it was beyond doubt that there were many struggles breaking out at this time that inspired people, and which were not associated with dictators, such as the Vietnam War and the civil rights movement in the US. Young Italians in particular were made aware there was an alternative to the lukewarm opposition that the Communist Party had led against the Christian Democrat government.

Some activists drew direct parallels between national liberation struggles in other countries and government repression in the south of Italy. In April 1969 the police opened fire on striking agricultural workers in the town of Battipaglia, south of Naples, killing two and wounding 50. There were chilling similarities with the 'Killing Fields' in Sicily twenty years earlier. So in a way it wasn't surprising that one response of the Che Club was to write wall slogans that told a basic truth: 'The police have killed again at Battipaglia'; but they also wrote: 'Arm the workers'.

Of course in one sense this was empty rhetoric – who was actually going to arm them? But in another way it was an illustration of the radical changes the Che Club wanted. Another time, the group spent a month painting a huge and detailed wall mural, showing Israeli warplanes bombing Palestinians.

All of this activity started to give people confidence. Pino Manzella, a giant of a man but nevertheless very softly spoken, recalls an encounter with one of the top *Mafiosi* of Cinisi:

It was the 1960s, my friend and I were 16 or 17 – long hair, the works – and one day the two of us went into a bar and saw Procopio Di Maggio in front of us. He looked us up and down and said to my friend: 'Why don't you cut your hair?' He replied: 'Why don't you mind your own business?' This was in a bar full of people. Di Maggio slapped him, my friend then went for him, but other people quickly separated them. Di Maggio didn't come out of this encounter very well but that wasn't really because he was attacked – it was because he wasn't respected. What happened then though was that the boy's father went to Di Maggio's house to apologise because he had this uncontrollable son who wouldn't respect people who should be respected.

My friend was part of the Che Guevara Club, so perhaps this was what led him to be perfectly at ease with what he had done, he wasn't afraid at all, he wasn't going to accept behaviour like that. Having said that, his father's actions probably covered his back.

Overall though, Peppino and others were beginning to provide a more tangible focus than just a newspaper. It was his friend and fellow activist Salvo Vitale who remembers that 'Peppino managed to give our group strength and coherence, forcing us outwards and into contact with real problems.' Although influenced by the extreme language of Maoism, the difference in Cinisi was that individuals such as Peppino wanted to get involved in campaigns that meant something to local people in the here and now. This is something also recognised by one of his arch enemies, fascist councillor Salvatore Maltese:

> What was Peppino's great strength? It was to gather around him some of the weakest people in society, people who had no role or purpose in many ways, lonely people, people who individually counted for nothing. The main way he did this was in the language he used in rallies, or demonstrations. If people showed any interest in what he was doing in public he would invite them to their meetings.

One of the first examples of concrete activity was a campaign for decent water supplies in nearby Terrasini.

Even today, particularly in the summer, in Sicily it is fairly common for taps to run dry. So they related to this intense frustration and managed to get a hundred women to demonstrate in front of the council – a very significant event in a town like Terrasini – carrying placards that read: 'the only decent water is in the mayor's villa'.

The core of the Che Club numbered about 25, but there were not just young people involved; the seed first planted with the *Socialist Idea* was starting to bear fruit. Not only was it a reference point for activists in other nearby towns, but many local peasants, trade unionists and building workers looked at what they said with considerable sympathy.

All the radical talk and intentions were put to the test when the issue of the airport resurfaced again.

The New Runway

When the authorities decided to build the airport back in the 1950s, one problem they had was getting their hands on the land that was needed, as it was owned by poor peasants. The system they used exposed the common interests of the powerful, be they *Mafiosi* or those acting in the name of democracy. A few Mafia landowners were given a high price for their land, so many illiterate peasants started queuing up to get the same deal. But once they had signed on the dotted line they discovered the amount they were due to be given – far less than the *Mafiosi* – would not even cover their solicitors' fees. The peasants who refused to sell, instinctively mistrusting the authorities, were then forced out under compulsory purchase orders, and eight to ten years later received financial compensation that again barely covered their legal costs. One of the people forced to sell some land was Felicia Impastato.

Apart from being notorious for corruption, Christian Democrat governments were also astoundingly inefficient. To start with, the new airport did not have either a waiting room or a control tower. Even more serious was the fact mentioned earlier: that the two east–west runways that opened in 1960 could not be used if there were strong sirocco winds blowing from the south. So a few years later the authorities started thinking about building a third runway.

Given the scandal associated with the original project, early preparations were shrouded in secrecy. The law said that any plan for compulsory purchases had to be publicised, so that people could appeal, even though they only had two weeks to do so. Nobody ever saw an announcement so nobody appealed. Therefore the first thing people knew about plans to build a new runway was when surveyors appeared one day and started taking measurements on peasants' lands.

So that history wouldn't repeat itself, the Communist and Socialist parties set up an 'Evictees' Committee'. Whereas the land used to build the first two runways ten years before had been largely uninhabited, about two hundred families lived in the area now designated for development, cultivating citrus groves and fruit orchards. In terms of employment and the provision of cheap agricultural produce, it was a vital economic resource for the town. Indeed, the building of the first two runways had already caused serious damage to Cinisi's economic infrastructure, destroying almost a third of all fertile and grazing land.

Peppino's group was also involved in this struggle; both these young radicals and the Evictees' Committee used to meet in a house due for demolition, owned by the family of Salvo Vitale. Like many Italians born during the Second World War, Vitale is somewhat short, probably as a result of lack of food as a baby. He speaks very slowly and deliberately, in a deep voice, and it was during this struggle that he became particularly close to Peppino – an intense but intermittent friendship that would last for many years. Given that he was in his final year at university, and was the local correspondent for *L'Ora*, a Palermo newspaper, the mainly illiterate peasants were always asking him to write articles, something he was happy to do.

Vitale explains one of the main reasons why the campaign had broad local support: 'The area of coastline due to be taken away was where everybody from Cinisi used to come in the summer. It was easy to learn how to swim there, because there were three rocks: the first was very near the shore, the second was at about head height, and when you reached the third this meant you had learnt how to swim.'

Even more important was the view of many local peasants that the whole idea of a third runway was a very risky proposition in any event. The new east-west runway would apparently be protected from the sirocco by mountains, but the wind still found its way down through gullies and small valleys, creating dangerous gusts and turbulence.

Protesters, meanwhile, faced a choice. They could receive some kind of compensation by applying through the Evictees' Committee, but most peasants had been bitten once before, so they were shy of going down that road again. This was why the majority supported Peppino and others, who argued for a militant campaign aimed at stopping the building of a third runway. As part of the campaign two demonstrations were held, and Peppino and four others were charged with organising one of them illegally, although charges were later dropped. But it was very symbolic that some of the poorest peasants of Cinisi marched up the Corso from their land near the sea, only to find the doors to the council chamber hurriedly shut in front of them. Peppino, still only 20, gave an impromptu speech in the courtyard.

Peasants had set up a system of alarms to warn each other when the bulldozers were coming. On 18 September 1968 the alarm went off and demonstrators hurried down to see three hundred police advancing over the existing runways, escorting bulldozers and other heavy equipment. When protesters came face to face with the police commander, he said to the men: 'The same old faces,' while he told the women, 'Housewives should be at home.' The peasants, vividly aware of what had happened ten years earlier, shouted 'Give us the money first,' and 'Where are we going to live if you knock our houses down?' The bulldozers rumbled forward and everyone lay down in front of them. They kept coming, but juddered to a halt at the feet of the protesters.

The police commander then sent his men in, who indiscriminately attacked men, women and children. A 70-year-old peasant suffered injuries to his head and ribs and was immediately taken to hospital. Franco Maniaci, who would later become deputy mayor of Cinisi, was arrested for shouting 'bastard' at a policeman. But there were too many demonstrators, so the bulldozers and the police gave up.

On a political level, though, things began to shift. It was around this time, Salvo Vitale recalls, that his editor at *L'Ora* in Palermo told him, 'there's no point in sending us any more articles because we're not going to publish them. The runway has got to be built.'

That same evening a 10-strong delegation went to meet regional government, and officials offered immediate payment of 10 per cent of the land's value. Given the elephantine slowness of Italian bureaucracy, this meant long-term starvation until the rest of the compensation arrived. The Evictees' Committee – or in other words the Communist and Socialist parties – accepted the agreement, whereas the majority of peasants did not. The militancy that had characterised these political parties just after the Second World War had ebbed over the years. Many Socialists and Communists had emigrated because there was no work, or had left anyway because the local establishment had told them there would be no work for people with their ideas.

Given that the 'official' opposition had thrown in the towel, the next morning the surveyors expected they could get on with their work undisturbed. But they found a hundred demonstrators opposing them, and once again the bulldozers were turned round. That evening protesters were warned: 'it would be better for you not to turn up tomorrow'. Yet a few did. Hundreds of police, plainclothes officers with cameras, police dogs – even a helicopter – confronted them.

There was a bitter smell as the bulldozers uprooted lemon trees. Peasant families cried as their houses were destroyed with all their furniture still inside. Now they had no land, no house and no money; they only started to receive compensation four years later. Many of the old people died of a broken heart soon after the destruction, a lot of young people either emigrated or were unemployed for many years.

Once the dust had settled, two things became clear: the town's economic lungs had been ripped out and the Mafia had consolidated its position. Overall, by now the airport had obliterated much of Cinisi's coastline and 40 per cent of productive land. People were therefore desperate for jobs and it was the Mafia that controlled the new ones created at the airport.

In the end, the peasants were proved right when they said the third runway would be dangerous. When the sirocco blows, aircraft are often rerouted to Catania airport. And on 5 May 1972 a DC9 crashed on the far side of Mount Pecoraro, killing 155 passengers. Two days before Christmas 1978 another DC9 crashed on approach out to sea, and 108 passengers drowned; on both occasions bad infrastructure as opposed to bad weather was blamed.

The Builders' Dispute

The campaign against the third runway was mainly aimed at the authorities. The next major public campaign – in support of local building workers – found local activists coming into direct conflict with the Mafia.

Unemployment has always been high in western Sicily, so there has invariably been a hungry local labour force that could potentially be exploited by unscrupulous employers. Like workers anywhere, what these people wanted was a decent wage and safe working conditions. The reality was that deaths at work were far higher than the number of Mafia murders: during the period 1971-75 an incredible 1,278 building workers died on the job, mainly through electrocution, collapsing scaffolding, or a whole range of accidents caused by tiredness. A working day of 10 to 12 hours was normal in the summer, with employers trying to keep the same level of exploitation going in the darker months through the use of floodlights. Workers were paid illegally, often at half the minimum wage rates.

This general situation was probably even more extreme in Cinisi. As we have seen, hundreds of families' homes had been destroyed just a few years earlier to build the third runway for Palermo airport. But those from a farming background were probably less familiar with Mafia domination of the town; it was something that they probably hadn't encountered regularly. Furthermore, the vast majority of the 400 or so building workers were under 25, and many must have been influenced by the climate of youth rebellion.

That was the situation for the workers. For the employers there were a variety of reasons that had caused this building boom – a bonanza that needed large numbers of new workers. One cause was migrants abroad sending money home, and their families deciding they wanted to live in better houses. Another was rich people in Palermo who wanted a second home by the sea. And the third cause was *Mafiosi* who had been enriched by the drugs trade and wanted a piece of the action – whether it be buildings for their personal use or simply making money on building work in general.

Leaving aside their own luxury accommodation, for the Mafia the system worked like this. First, *Mafiosi* had contacts and influence within the council's building and planning committees – they could apply pressure and decide which areas would be set aside for building work, and snap that land up cheaply before the decision became publicly known. The price of the land would then rise enormously and they could sell it off at a huge profit. Alternatively, they could contract a company to erect a building at a cost of say 12 million lire, but then sell the completed property at 25 million to the many hopeful buyers looking to invest. Linked to all of this was the local council, which was often prepared to turn a blind eye if regulations were flouted, in return for a backhander or for a nice bundle of votes at election time. Besides this rather haphazard market there was another huge area of building work: the construction of the Palermo-Trapani motorway, which passed through Cinisi.

There was another quite fundamental reason why no building company could avoid dealing with the Mafia: they had a stranglehold over the supply of raw materials – hard core, cement, sand, tiles, marble and fittings. And while it was virtually physically impossible to use heavy supplies or equipment from outside the area, if companies did try to use non-Mafia suppliers they frequently found their sites suffered mysterious fires or bomb attacks; the dynamite used within Mafia-controlled quarries could easily be put to other uses outside. And if these small building companies and their owners did anything else the Mafia disapproved of, they could stop supplying them with these essential goods and create serious problems for them. In one way or another all building work was closely connected to the Mafia.

It was a sign of the increasing maturity of Peppino and his group that they were able to work with the CGIL union federation, despite the fact that this union was closely allied to the Communist Party. Historically the CGIL had been a militant union, and many members were still very radical, so this local collaboration may well have happened because the Communist Party was no longer interested in leading militant struggles. Pino Vitale, a short and straight-talking electrician who worked at the airport and was a union activist, recalls the dispute beginning for the following reason: 'It started because Napoleone, a building worker and member of the Communist Party, couldn't really get his party interested.'

Demanding better pay and conditions for hundreds of building workers meant working towards a situation where these people didn't feel obliged to work under Mafia conditions – in broader terms this is one of the basic changes that needs to be made to remove the influence of organised crime. Therefore a union leaflet was distributed demanding an end to casualisation:

> Building workers – our working and living conditions have always suffered from the most inhuman exploitation. The majority of us has never been on the books, never had

any help with illnesses or accidents, has always worked in unsafe and unhealthy conditions – without insurance.

Now is the time to bring this to an end! We are getting organised to demand our rights and satisfy our needs. This is what we want:

1) Hiring to be carried out legally.
2) The 40 hour week to be respected.
3) Appropriate payment of overtime (35 per cent extra).

The impact was huge, as Pino Vitale remembers: 'The fact that these workers were insisting they be put on the books was something almost unheard of in Cinisi.' But they went further, as he explains: 'We put up a poster denouncing the involvement of the local job centre in sending people to those jobs. The manager was a fascist, who afterwards had to resign.' These young activists were no longer just shouting the odds about Marx or Mao; they were starting to make changes in the town.

From just a few individuals trying to organise workers into gaining their rights, by the end of 1973 several meetings had been held, and there was a group of 90–100 young building workers committed to fighting for their rights. The demands they were making were threatening the entire structure of economic and social power in the town; in essence they wanted to transfer a significant amount of wealth from unscrupulous employers and *Mafiosi* to ordinary working people.

The Mafia weren't going to ignore all this. Piero Impastato, another activist and distant relative of Peppino, recalls: 'I remember I once went with Peppino to a meeting he held with about 50 building workers at the airport, and as he was speaking Giuseppe Finazzo walked in. Not only did he have his own building company, he was also Badalamenti's right-hand man. He just looked around, he had only turned up to see who was there.'

Who knows whether Peppino realised that history was virtually repeating itself? Twenty-five years earlier, in 1948, the Communist Stefano Venuti had experienced almost exactly the same kind of indirect intimidation from Mafia boss Procopio Di Maggio, in a similar situation with workers trying to win their legal rights. The key turning point came when a leaflet was produced calling a demonstration outside the council building in a week's time.

Suddenly the parents of many of the young building workers started getting knocks on the door. When they opened them they were told: 'You'd better watch out for your son, he's mixing with bad company, he could end up getting hurt.' Who was making the threats? According to Pino Vitale:

> Pressure was applied on families either by the employers, or by the Mafia. Parents would then say to their sons: 'Now that you've got involved with the Communists, you'll never work again'. This was a real worry for people from an agricultural background, because after the building of the third runway many of them were forced to emigrate. Some people had even died of a broken heart because they had lost the very land that had allowed them to raise an entire family.

Whether the employers were closely linked to the Mafia or not didn't really matter – what mattered was the reality of capitalism, as Vitale explains: 'You couldn't prove employers were linked to the Mafia. But they were all in competition with each other, and they all tried to lower their costs.' And by the same token, people were frightened for two different reasons: fear of the Mafia and fear of losing their job.

That was the 'scattergun' approach to workers and their families. Another approach was to target individual activists such as Peppino Impastato by sending them threatening letters. Pino Vitale also received one of these letters:

> We're writing you this letter to tell you something. Above all we're telling you a friend of yours (Impastato) has already received a letter like this. We are people who earn our daily bread and you Communists want to take it away from us. But we're telling you and all Communists to lay

off the builders. We're ready to do anything if you carry on we'll act straight away. And we're not afraid because many political forces are behind us. You, Impastato and others have played games with us builders. So now we've decided to blow up the house where you have your club and then it'll be your turn. So lay off the builders once and for all and let us get on with our work. If we get to hear lots of things about you and we've got spies who tell us then we'll start threatening again. It's not us who exploits the lads but it's you lot who keep on causing aggro! Now we're watching everything you do so be careful the whole lot of you not to make any false moves.

Goodbye, and watch what you're doing with the builders.

A group of workers

Threats to blow up a building, in a town where the local Mafia boss had been murdered in a car bomb just a few years earlier, were chillingly realistic. The precise comments relating to Pino Vitale's activities contained in this second letter could only convince him he was being closely watched:

We've been told that you're a Communist too. You've been warned to lay off the builders but instead you've made up leaflets and we've seen you. You're going to pay for this you have to stop fuckin' bothering us. You've got to pack it in and from now on you're going to pay for it. We'll take action personally against you or the house where you go with the builders. You've got a job what the fuck are you interested in the builders for why don't you stop turning builders into Communists. Anyway from now on you're all going to pay students Communists builders. As soon as we move we're sure you'll lay off the builders.

Down with the Communists

A group of workers

The bad language, both in the sense of swearwords and poor grammar, makes the letters seem like genuine threats. They could have been written by some of the 'reputable' small building companies or by *Mafiosi* – there was no way of knowing. Not only were the Mafia more than capable of carrying out these threats, very few people felt the police would investigate seriously or could offer meaningful protection.

The campaign quickly collapsed. The demonstration planned outside the council building was called off. Many people involved in the campaign then had to engage in the schizophrenic communication used in Mafia towns. They endured a painful ritual of pretending they didn't know fellow activists when they met them. By openly ignoring friends, frightened campaigners were trying to send a public message to the people who were threatening them that they had stopped working together.

It was clearly a defeat for these young activists. But this was now the second broad campaign in which they had played a leading role, and this one had threatened the economic interests of some *Mafiosi*. The stakes had been raised on both sides – but what caused Peppino to become such a committed anti-Mafia campaigner at such a young age?

The Impastato Brothers: One Down, One to Go

Peppino turned 20 in 1968. Perhaps it was the tensions in his family life that led him to both study far more than most other people, and on a personal level to be rather withdrawn and serious. He had enrolled at Palermo University in 1966 and started to take courses but two years later many universities in Italy and around the world were in turmoil. Peppino later looked back on that period thus: '1968 caught me by surprise. I took part in the early student struggles and occupations chaotically. And once again, I came to agree with the ideas of one of the groups more on an emotional than a political level.'

He is painfully honest with himself – part of his interest in politics was the search for an emotional substitute for his disturbed family life. He once wrote a poem in his diary:

A long dividing wall
So long you cannot see the end
A chorus of yellowed skulls:
'We shall not have love'

Leaving all these personal considerations aside, Peppino and others were deadly serious about turning the world upside down, and to do that they had to agree on how that would be done. So, not surprisingly, there was a lot of discussion about what kind of organisation and party was needed. As he says, this was: 'a time of arguments about the party – what it meant and how it should be built. It was an amazing and fascinating period of theoretical discussion.' But it was also difficult for him: 'I didn't speak to anyone for days, then when I came up with new ideas I became happy again. I was going through a period of uncontrollable schizophrenia.'

For several years after 1968 Peppino and others joined, left and created a whole range of local and national political parties and organisations. Once again he reveals the schizophrenic nature of his life, defining this period: 'Maybe this was the most heartbreaking and exciting time of my life and of my political activity.'

His mother, who didn't see him nearly as much as she would have liked, used to worry:

> He didn't accept this society, he used to study all the time. My brother, who was well off, allowed him to keep studying because he paid his fees and his living expenses, everything. He had his head into politics, he hardly thought about anything else.
>
> Sometimes I would ask him: 'Peppino, what do you do in the evenings?' And he'd answer: 'Nothing, I kill time.' And I'd answer him: 'Don't get into trouble. You know you can't do that.' 'Why can't I do that?' 'Because you belong to a Mafia family – and you can't act on what you're saying.'

Felicia was trying to face two ways at the same time: looking after her son and being a dutiful wife to her Mafia husband. But she was trying to reconcile what could not be reconciled; despite the fact she was both mother and wife she couldn't bring her family together. It was unthinkable that Luigi Impastato would change his Mafia ways, so as long as Peppino carried on with his political activity nobody would have a normal family life.

The only time Luigi Impastato really worried about his son's activities was before local council elections. His mother remembers that Luigi would ask his son to come round and tell him:

> 'You know the elections are on, careful what you get up to, don't talk about the Mafia. If you had got a degree, my friends would have . . .' 'Your friends? You think I want a job from them? I'd rather die of hunger than take a job from one of your friends.' They used to shout at each other . . . He'd tell him to his face: 'They disgust me, I can't stand them.' . . . So then he said: 'get out'.

So she was forced to have a secret relationship with her son, almost as if they were illicit lovers, and would literally watch the clock when he came round:

> Giovanni was at the shop with his father and Peppino and I were at home by ourselves. I used to run a bath for him, always on the quiet. I'd say to him: 'Get a move on!' He finished his bath, put on his clean clothes and left. Or he used to come round to eat, when I got his lunch ready for 1pm. I used to bung the pasta in and set the table: meat, fruit. 'Get a move on, in case your dad comes.' He would finish eating and leave.

Indeed when they used to argue about Peppino, Luigi would sometimes say to his wife: 'You're married to your son!' Even without Peppino in the house, and the best efforts of Felicia, the tension was tremendous. As she explains: 'My husband's relatives used to tell him what Peppino was doing . . . they couldn't stand him'.

As is so often the case, Giovanni stood in the shadow of his older brother. He had a stark choice in front of him:

either behave like his father or like his brother. While he never took on his father's views, in his adolescence he never made exactly the same kind of choices that Peppino had. Although Giovanni nearly always speaks in calm and measured tones, he is as brutally honest about himself as his brother is:

> I was part of the group that Peppino managed to organise at the end of the 1960s, even though I never had a leading role. We had a love-hate relationship, because we had completely different personalities. He had studied much more than me, and knew a lot more. He was also much more extrovert, whereas I was still a teenager. I had a girlfriend, I used to go dancing, I liked to have a good time.
>
> Peppino and I didn't live together for a long time, it was just one phase of our lives. Yet after he was kicked out of the house I always felt the absence of my brother strongly. But we would meet up outside – and I always shared his ideas and political decisions.
>
> I had a good relationship with my mum but not with my father, it annoyed me he had kicked Peppino out of the house. I had already worked out he was a *Mafioso*, and I didn't share his values or his way of behaving. He was very authoritarian towards me, he wasn't open to any discussion with me. He simply tried to impose his values and lifestyle on his sons. The problem is that he couldn't really convince us – at the end of the day a *Mafioso* isn't used to in-depth discussion. He simply tried to impose himself on us, and this really annoyed Peppino because he could see he was living with the Mafia.

Although they might be crude and violent, one thing *Mafiosi* aren't is stupid. Giovanni's father understood that he had 'lost' Peppino, but also that his younger son was different, and here he saw an opening to apply classic Mafia pressure, as Giovanni relates:

> He understood I didn't have the same dynamic and adventurous character as Peppino, he could see I was

much more docile and soft. To some extent his tactics worked because I was a bit afraid. He often warned me: 'be careful', adding that if I went the same way as my brother I could lose everything. If I did what he told me to he could guarantee me a life without any problems. All of this was going on when I was 18 or 19, and he was sure of himself. Even though he knew I agreed with Peppino, and didn't agree with him, he was sure that I would never betray him, and never leave home like he did.

One of the key arguments used by the Mafia is respect for traditional family values. Giovanni accepted this, but not because he agreed with his father's attitudes. As he explains, much of his thinking came out consideration for his mother and brother: 'Although he dominated me there was another reason I behaved like this – I wanted to keep a minimum level of contact with him to try and limit the damage Peppino's traumatic situation had created within the family. So I tried to compromise and keep things on an even keel.'

To the extent that these three members of the Impastato family lived together, Giovanni's line of thinking worked. Yet while the good ship Impastato may have more or less kept an even keel, Peppino was outside rocking it furiously, and the boat itself was adrift in a stormy sea of Mafia activity.

9

Capo of the Commission

The Return of the Commission

The 'Commission' had been set up on the advice of Italian-American gangsters way back in 1957. An organisation such as the Mafia, based in a society rapidly changing from farming to industry and services, needed to move with the times. Things had to be organised, coordinated, agreed upon. Criminal activities such as drug or cigarette smuggling, or large building projects, required very considerable amounts of money, so 'joint ventures' between rival gangs were needed, as were banks – and in this period many new banks were founded with Mafia money.

But then came the First Mafia War of 1962-63, culminating in the massacre of seven policemen. The Italian establishment woke up from its slumber and had to be seen to be doing something against the Mafia. Consequently, over a hundred people faced the first ever 'maxi trial' held in Catanzaro, but when the verdict was reached in December 1968, 114 out of 141 *Mafiosi* were cleared, including Tano Badalamenti, who was acquitted *in absentia* because he was on the run. A few leaders were given long sentences but most defendants were released because they had already spent a long period in jail.

So by early 1969 the coast was clear again, and Badalamenti duly resurfaced in July. But none of these shrewd leaders would have broken cover if another condition hadn't been created: a *pax mafiosa* – Mafia peace. Lots of people had seen their best friends or family members gunned down, and if anybody thought people were still harbouring grudges none of these wily old foxes would have ever crept out of the undergrowth.

Major gang leaders organised summit meetings. At one held in a Zurich hotel all the main bosses sat round and talked lots of issues through. Nearly all agreed with the slogans that were bandied about: 'Peace, peace, peace! Let's stop all the murders and move forward.' Yet one boss didn't utter a word throughout the entire discussion, Salvatore 'Little Bird' Greco. At the end he said: 'You're making peace – do what you want – you're the majority.' It was clear that he mistrusted many of the people in the room but accepted that it was pointless to set himself against everyone else.

Greco's suspicions were soon justified. There was a huge shoot-out in December 1969 in which five *Mafiosi* died. But rather than the start of a new war it was really the end of the First Mafia War – the last score had been settled. The sign that things had moved on was that all major families contributed to the manpower needed for the strike force, led by a man from the town of Corleone, Totò Riina. In a climate of unity, but in perennial distrust of each other, the gangs moved forward.

Representatives, or leaders, went to these summit meetings – yet what did they represent? It almost goes without saying that they represented gangs, but what defines a gang, or family? Where does one end and the other begin?

Apart from blood links, what defines a Mafia gang is territorial control. The gang and their leader must have a physical presence, the existence of the Mafia is based on it being tangible although rarely visible, most of the time it is in your mind not in your eyes. So, once a group of people gain control of an area they become a gang. And to get in that position, they must have a fearsome reputation that intimidates everybody, to the extent that in reality they very rarely have to use violence. Controlling an area means earning a rake-off from all economic activities within it. If any gang wants to do anything in another one's area they have to ask for permission. In short, controlling a territory means control over most of the legal and all of the illegal activities that are carried out there.

This is why somebody like Gaetano Badalamenti became one of the three men to lead the new Commission. Don Tano had been boss in Cinisi since 1963 and partly thanks to him the town was experiencing a boom – most of it due to the drugs trade. If money was flowing in then Badalamenti was bound to be popular, and therefore could impose his control over the area fairly easily.

Gaspare Cucinella remembers how he noticed these changes and what it meant for people who opposed the Mafia:

> Suddenly, out of the blue, people came back from the States and started saying, 'take a trip to America, go on a trip to the States!' Don Tano developed a system that couldn't fail because people had so many relatives over there. Cinisi became a boomtown and people were saying: 'God bless Don Tano'. People were building villas and all sorts. And this is why whoever spoke out against the Mafia was a shithead.

Many local people, often women, became drug mules, flying from the local airport apparently to visit relatives in the United States. Felicia Impastato recalled some of the sociological changes the drugs boom produced:

> They never stopped. They came and went, came and went. One of them built a villa, and had a four-million-lira chandelier installed. What an ignoramus! Who is going to be visiting them – it's not as if they ever organised huge society receptions. Four million! And whoever goes to

visit them says: 'Isn't this chandelier beautiful?' 'It cost four million'. And these people want to pay any price for my cousin's land, given that it's near to theirs.

Peasant families were building luxury villas. In just a few years some people moved from cohabiting with animals to living in accommodation with the most expensive fittings.

Back in the centre of town this huge influx of money could be seen as well – by the early 1970s Cinisi was second only to Milan in terms of density of car ownership. Not many people could fail to see the shiny luxury cars parked outside the houses of *Mafiosi*, and news quickly spread about where the money had come from. After a lifetime, or even generations, of poverty, people flaunted their wealth, as Felicia describes: 'everybody had their balconies open, and was sitting out. Others passed by in cars, others would walk around, because it's a small town.' A few years later it emerged that over half of Cinisi families had a second car, and one-third had a house in the country.

According to the supergrass Antonino Calderone, by early 1970:

> Gaetano Badalamenti became the most important person within Cosa Nostra. One of his first actions was to organise a series of attacks in Sicily to show everybody that the Mafia was back, stronger than ever. He often used to say: 'We've got to bring Sicily back under our control. We've got to make ourselves heard. We've to chuck all policemen into the sea.'

This is strategic thinking. Badalamenti saw that the Mafia had to create its own special brand of 'public relations'. One way they announced their return was by exploding a bomb inside the Appeal Court buildings in Catania. The murder of an investigative journalist in 1970 and Judge Pietro Scaglione the following year were further signs of growing confidence and power. This latter murder was something quite rare and dangerous – a direct attack on a senior government figure – but Badalamenti quickly changed tack and tried to stop any head-on attacks on other important government figures.

One of the reasons was that the Mafia was now an important player, not so much in the corridors of power, but in the back rooms. In the front rooms, or command centres of power, there was a lot of unease in the late 1960s. A mass student movement had exploded in 1968 and, far more worryingly, this had detonated a wave of general strikes. In France President de Gaulle temporarily fled the country at the height of the 1968 general strike, while in Italy fascists and their supporters within government had even taken the first steps towards launching a military coup in June 1964. Indeed in the summer of 1970 Tommaso Buscetta, Luciano Leggio and 'Little Bird' Greco held a series of meetings in Italy and Switzerland to discuss whether to support a right-wing coup, which in the end never really took off. Nevertheless, it was an indication both of how powerful the Mafia was, and that politicians knew where to find its leaders and were prepared to talk to them.

In late 1973 Badalamenti's power increased even further; he was either elected as sole leader of the Commission after a vote at a summit, or simply declared himself leader. Either way, he was now boss of the Mafia, the *capo di tutti i capi.*

Although most gangs tended to do their own thing, there were some joint ventures in this period, particularly cigarette smuggling. The system was centred on Naples and was run by the criminal organisation dominant in that city, the Camorra. Nevertheless, much of the capital needed to start up and maintain the trade came from the Mafia. Most major Sicilian families invested in the trade and reaped handsome profits. But the power structure was clear: in the words of a supergrass, after all expenses were paid 'everything was added up, and the profits were taken to Gaetano Badalamenti, who then divided the money up for everybody.'

Totò Riina and the *Corleonesi*

As is often the case in Mafia history, too much power above leads to resentment below.

In the world of the Mafia, as elsewhere, power tends to come from wealth, and in the 1970s Sicily was flooded by drug money. Sicilian *Mafiosi* were well placed to develop a global system: they had a long history of links with producing countries so they could source the morphine base quite easily. And it was in Sicily that they did the refining because they felt the police wouldn't create too many problems for them. Once that was done, Sicilians had thousands of personal contacts in the States, to whom they exported roughly 80 per cent of all refined heroin supplies through family links. This was the period when a global drug system emerged on a large scale; between 1974 and 1982 the amount of heroin seized around the world rose by six and a half times.

To the extent that anyone follows any rules within the Mafia, Badalamenti should have offered other gangs a 'piece of the action' in the drugs trade, but, as ever, in practice a *Mafioso* is selfish and cannot be trusted. Besides, given the long prison sentences that people risked, drug deals were not openly discussed at summit meetings. Badalamenti could justify himself by arguing that what he was really doing was sending drugs to the United States from his own territory – the airport – therefore he wasn't obliged to involve anyone else.

Totò Riina, an up-and-coming killer and boss from the inland town of Corleone, was resentful of Badalamenti's wealth and power. Riina and many of the Corleonesi had still not made a full move to Palermo and had missed out on making big money. Up until the mid-1960s, beyond Palermo most *Mafiosi* concentrated on low-level extortion and protection rackets. Indeed Riina, unusually moved to tears, once told a supergrass that when he was in prison in 1966–67 he was still so poor that his mother didn't have enough money to come and visit him.

What infuriated Riina and others was that Badalamenti never mentioned what he was up to, they only found out from other sources. Because Badalamenti wouldn't play ball with them, the Corleonesi thought up another way of getting rich quickly – kidnapping wealthy people. The first victim was taken in 1971, Pino Vassallo, son of the main building contractor who had profited from the 'sack of Palermo'. By any standards of strategic thinking this was crazy: the Corleonesi were directly attacking the business and power structure they fed off, the Christian-Democrat-dominated public sector. But Riina and his men kept to their guns, and after five months got an incredible sum, the equivalent of £4 billion today. And what they did with much of this ransom was very shrewd strategically speaking – they distributed much of it to the poorer gangs in Palermo. Naturally this wasn't an act of generosity, it was the beginning of their long-term strategy to gain new loyal friends, and to undermine Badalamenti and his allies.

Another victim was selected the following year, Luciano Cassina. Totò Riina conducted negotiations personally over the phone, sometimes while physically sitting on his victim. Up to £9.2 million in today's money was paid to release Cassina, and was collected by Mafia priest Agostino Coppola. This time around the Corleonesi kept the money. Like any capitalist enterprise, they needed to invest large amounts of money to start up in business, and that business was the drugs trade. Their first move was to ask the Catania family to take part in a joint venture, and naturally the Corleonesi behaved the same as Badalamenti, telling nobody about it.

Riina had sprung this kidnap when Badalamenti and other leaders were in jail, yet even so he denied all knowledge of it when Badalamenti came out and asked him about it. Mafia wisdom had it that if rich or important people were kidnapped, the police would take such a crime seriously and start searching and arresting people all over the island, thus disturbing *all* Mafia activities. Badalamenti's view was: 'We can't declare war on the state', and he made it clear there were to be no more kidnappings. The Corleonesi pretended to agree, and then waited a short while before carrying out a few more.

By far the most serious kidnapping took place in July 1975. Luigi Corleo was father-in-law of the fantastically rich Nino Salvo, millionaire tax collector and close friend of Christian Democrats and Gaetano Badalamenti. While never admitting to anything, the Corleonesi were in fact demanding an impossibly high price, £120 billion at today's prices. Although Corleo was probably the richest man in Sicily, Nino Salvo turned to his Mafia friends, who told him they knew nothing. As the weeks wore on, and Corleo's death became a certainty due to the fact he was well over 70, Salvo pleaded with Badalamenti to his face, begging him to at least find the body of the old man. Once again, Badalamenti could do nothing – and this was an intense embarrassment for him.

For Riina it was the opposite: in the words of a supergrass he was sending a message 'as big as a house' to anybody who would listen that he was fast emerging as a rival to Don Tano.

Yet for all of this jockeying for power, which took place over several years, the agreed position remained that Badalamenti was in charge. One *Mafioso* once described Badalamenti thus: 'a crude and ignorant person, but in Mafia circles he is "revered as a god that walks the earth".'

A Mafia God Walks the Earth

The high point of Badalamenti's career came with his 'Pizza Connection' system in the United States – the distribution of hard drugs through pizza parlours. At one stage in the early 1980s Caribbean banks were getting so overloaded with the dirty money they needed to launder that the whole operation became bottlenecked. There was so much cash that delivering money in suitcases became impractical, so private jets were chartered to transport millions of dollars.

It was a global operation. From the global east came the heroin, from the global west – Bolivia and Paraguay – came the cocaine. Heroin was generally refined in Sicily, but in

Italy most drug users lived in the richer cities of the north and centre of the country (where the drugs were originally delivered). In any event, most of the heroin was refined and sent on to a country in the global north, the United States.

Despite such a huge operation Badalamenti's wealth and power still had geographical foundations, he still needed a physical base, his own 'home turf'. If he didn't have these things he would have counted for nothing in the Mafia pecking order. The only problem he had as regards Cinisi was getting there as often as he wanted, given that sometimes he was either forced to live elsewhere in Italy in 'internal exile', or was in jail awaiting trials that either never happened or in which he was acquitted. Yet when he did appear, he always made an impression, as Piero Impastato recalls: 'Badalamenti had an amazing physical presence. He reminded me a lot of that actor who always used to play Dracula – Christopher Lee.'

In one way or another it was virtually impossible not to be aware of Badalamenti's change in status, *Mafiosi* made no attempts to hide it. As a town councillor explains, they would also boast about having links with one of the most senior Christian Democrat politicians, who had already been prime minister three times:

> When somebody becomes head of the Commission their house becomes a port of call for people from all over the island. Gaetano Badalamenti's house used to be frequented by ordinary people, then at a certain point certain well-known individuals were always going in and out of it. There were loads of Mercedes and BMWs parked outside, whereas virtually everyone else had little Fiat 500s. I remember I used to go into bars during that period and people were saying: 'these days Gaetano Badalamenti has got top-level friends in Rome, he's a friend of Andreotti'. People would turn round and say: 'What? Andreotti?' Today maybe it would be dangerous to say something like that, but back then it was something that was said openly, with pride.

Badalamenti's main meeting place was the Palazzolo bar, which significantly was in front of the council building. And as one of his opponents was forced to recognise: 'Whenever Badalamenti went to a bar he was always surrounded by loads of people, people who were desperate in one way or another.' Badalamenti and his gang could supply the commodity that people in town were most desperate for, and it wasn't drugs – it was jobs.

One of the many people who couldn't stand him was Felicia Impastato, but as she says:

> It was my husband who told me we had to go to Don Tano's house out of courtesy, when Peppino was already making his accusations. I didn't want to go, and every time we used to argue about it. But his wife had been asking about us, and it always used to make my husband happy. Badalamenti's house was always full of people – and what a queue there was outside his door! And how could I ever forget the luxury – two people used to come from Palermo to clean Badalamenti's Persian carpets. I remember once we were talking and somebody asked me: 'What's your son, a Maoist?' So I told him, 'everyone's got their own party. You've got your own one, and he and his friends have got another one. Everybody's got their own.'

Nowadays Badalamenti never even asked after Felicia's son Peppino. Maybe this was because he had more important things on his mind, or maybe he was simply too angry about Peppino's activities.

10

Crazy Waves

Maybe Badalamenti's henchman was right to call Peppino Impastato a Maoist. While Peppino and others were simply unaware that Mao was a brutal dictator, they were nevertheless committed revolutionary socialists, people who believed that fundamental change could not come through parliamentary politics and parties. Locally, they had seen all the major parties slowly moving towards direct or indirect accommodation with the Mafia. So their aim was still the creation of a mass national movement outside parliament, concentrating on where people were collectively strong – principally where they worked.

But by the early 1970s – after several years of intense political activity – Peppino's generation could see that the revolution wasn't round the corner. So without changing their ideas, they started to take seriously issues such as local and national elections. In 1972 Peppino took part in the general election campaign built around a left-wing newspaper, *Il Manifesto*. The results weren't that encouraging, but Peppino more than others became increasingly convinced that the comfortable set-up at Cinisi council needed to be challenged.

Given that they really didn't have the experience or forces to mount their own campaign, in the same year Peppino and his group decided to put their votes behind the Communist Party, the only left-wing force standing in local council elections. They had very little faith in the enthusiastically parliamentary Communist Party, what they wanted perhaps more than anything else was for people to see there was at least some kind of alternative to the sleazy Christian Democrats.

Soon after the election they were shocked. The sole Communist councillor they had helped to elect repaid them by joining a coalition with the Christian Democrats and became deputy mayor. It was the hypocrisy of the Communists that they found so irritating. In the same period in which their councillor was in alliance with the Christian Democrats, the local branch wrote an article in its area magazine entitled: 'Is Capitalism's Crisis Caused by the Oil Crisis?' which contained the following conclusion: 'It's clear that the struggle will not be easy and will not develop in a linear fashion, but today it has never been clearer that socialism is the only real solution to the intrinsic anarchy of the capitalist system.' How could the party face two directions at the same time, talking about socialism while sharing power with the traditional facilitators of Italian capitalism? All of this caused a lot of bitterness, which was to last until the Communist Party dissolved itself in the 1990s.

So Peppino decided that revolutionaries should stand on their own platform. In 1976 he was a candidate in regional elections for a revolutionary party called Lotta Continua (Continuous Struggle), obtaining 4 per cent of the vote and the highest number of personal preference votes out of all candidates – 350.

One of the reasons he was so successful was that he had become a very popular public speaker. Sometimes up to a thousand people came to Peppino's campaign speeches, an incredible number in a town of around ten thousand people. As Piero Impastato says, people came to listen not just because he had a good style of speaking: 'Many people used to come to hear his speeches, even right wingers and *Mafiosi*, who would either listen or blow raspberries. The real reason though was that Peppino named names – both politicians and *Mafiosi*. If you stop and think, though, this was the early 1970s – how did he manage to do that?' It took a lot of courage to stand up against the political and criminal establishment of the town, but Peppino did it. Another member of his group, Pino Manzella, concurs: 'Loads of people came to hear Peppino speak. People were curious to hear what names he named. And the way he used to talk was like a bulldozer.'

But Peppino and the others were not interested in becoming dull and unimaginative local politicians. While a few of them stood in elections, they still wanted to create an active campaigning group. The idea they developed was to appeal to young people on a cultural level primarily, rather than concentrate immediately on ideology.

No Sex, No Drugs, Some Rock 'n' Roll

It was the 'Summer of Love' in 1967; people were going to San Francisco and wearing flowers in their hair. But in towns like Cinisi it was still winter. Girls couldn't go out unaccompanied and had to wear sensible clothes, young men wore jackets and ties and cut their hair short. Felicetta Vitale looks back at the difficulties young people had back then:

> It was very difficult for boys and girls to meet, you used to have go somewhere where nobody could see you because you couldn't meet up publicly. For a boy and girl to be seen together in public, talking together on the Corso was seen as a provocation by their parents.
>
> So you'd get criticised at home – sometimes they would stop you from going out in the evenings – obviously this only happened to girls, not boys. And to avoid these problems you had to meet up in the back streets. One of the favourite places was behind the church, because not many people lived round there.

Traditional Catholicism was strong. In most Italian schools religious education was taught by priests, and to prepare for their first communion and confirmation most Italian children had to go to Sunday school. Entertainment and holidays were often run by the Church, local churches organised holiday outings for poor families, run by priests or local volunteers.

Many towns also had a cinema run by the Church. The sequence in the film *Cinema Paradiso*, set in the Sicily of the 1950s, where the young film operator Salvatore discovers all the scenes censored by the priest from classic films, was very close to reality. Growing up as a boy in Terrasini in the 1950s, Salvo Vitale recalls: 'I can remember going to church once and seeing the priest with a list of films, categorised as "for everyone", "for adults" and "banned". And priests would openly tell you which films you were and weren't allowed to see. I clearly remember one Neapolitan film, *Core 'ngrato*, was banned because there was a kiss in it.' Some young Italians who had grown up in the 1970s only realised that there was a dance scene between Olivia Newton John and John Travolta at the end of *Grease* when they watched it on television many years later, because priests cut the scene due to the 'provocative' clothing and behaviour.

For decades there had been no serious challenge to the Church's self-appointed role of guardian of public morals. For example, in 1951 there were 48 marriages performed with a religious ceremony in Cinisi and just six without; in 1974 there were 64 religious ceremonies and just two civil ceremonies.

Individuals such as Peppino Impastato were not just breaking from the Mafia, they were also challenging these restrictive traditions. So another revolutionary input from this young group of activists, as Pino Manzella recalls, was trying to date girls in a 'modern' way. The tradition that dominated at that time was that girls only went out in public if they were escorted by relatives. For a boy and a girl to go out together, the boy needed to ask permission from her parents. Peppino, Pino and others started actively to disobey this unwritten rule, and although they weren't spectacularly successful, discovered that many girls looked upon their efforts with sympathy. So although 'the Summer of Love' never arrived in Cinisi, by the late 1960s winter was turning to spring.

One of the collective moments when many of these rules were disobeyed was during the period of Carnival, in mid-February. For a few days Cinisi would be 'turned upside down' and normal conventions abandoned, particularly those stopping men from mixing with women. People would dress up in costumes, open their front doors to strangers and allow people to dance together. Confetti would be thrown around the street, and some people would drink a lot. On one memorable occasion the wife of the actor Gaspare Cucinella came out on her balcony and yelled at her drunken husband to come home. His provocative response was almost a complaint: 'If it wasn't for you, I would be full of alcohol and syphilis.' Not that all conventions disappeared at Carnival: women still had to be 'protected' by men. If they were to go into the houses of strangers and dance they had to be masked, and there had to be an unmasked man to escort them who would knock at the door of a house, and if his voice was recognised the door would be opened.

Reality would sometimes intrude on people's enjoyment. Gaspare Cucinella recalled what happened one year:

> Gaetano Badalamenti couldn't stand the sight of me because I always took the mickey out of him. One evening during Carnival, when people used to go from one house to another, dancing and so on, I was walking down the Corso with my wife and he was coming up it with his. And he said to me: 'get out of my way and let me through'. I just answered: 'why don't you get out of my way?' We could have stayed there the whole night, but he moved out of way. Why did he do this? One of my uncles was a friend of his, so he didn't want to offend him.

These were the moments when extrovert and imaginative people such as Gaspare Cucinella became close to Peppino, who once wrote a bittersweet poem about Carnival:

Today we throw our masks off
By masking ourselves.
Carnival is a very strange festival:
Hypocrisy is defeated
By making a masked monument to it.
Tonight I want to cut up all of my feelings
Into a thousand coloured confetti.
Then I will throw them at the throng of revellers
To brighten up their dancing.

Along with new ideas, new technologies were starting to circulate. In Partinico, Giuseppe Nobile recalls: 'In 1975 the first person ever talked to me about videotapes – it was Peppino – at the time I didn't even know what they were!' Although widespread use of videos was still several years off, Peppino showed video footage several times when he stood as a candidate in spring 1976.

In a practical sense, Peppino's cultural horizons were broadened by what was happening in nearby Terrasini. Starting in autumn 1974, for the next two years young people ran an experimental but popular theatre group, having created a stage of 40 square metres and an auditorium of 150 seats within a larger public building. This same group then launched a series of weekly alternative film showings in early 1975, which were always followed by a public debate. Peppino came and took part in nearly all of them.

This experience encouraged him to set up the Music and Culture Club in Cinisi in 1976. The core of this group was between 10 and 15 people, and they organised film shows, concerts, theatre activities, photographic exhibitions. The most popular events were the film shows: the meeting room would fill with up to 100 people. One of the reasons it was popular was because it was a place where young men and women could socialise. Two young people who met at Music and Culture were Peppino's younger brother Giovanni and Felicetta Vitale. A small but very determined woman, she and Giovanni would act as a team in all their battles over the coming decades:

I really got involved with politics through Music and Culture, and with the feminist collective that grew up within it. So I took part in meetings, debates and so on. And Peppino always encouraged us women to get active and start speaking in public; Fanny Vitale, Pino Manzella's wife, was the first one to speak at a rally.

We moved on to debates with women's groups that came from Palermo. What we really wanted was that ordinary people – housewives – came and discussed women's issues, such as abortion and divorce. We had a very direct approach: 'come on, get involved!' There was a big debate within the group about how to approach people, and I for one felt that if you related to people aggressively you would alienate them. I disagreed with the idea of saying: 'we don't want anything to do with men, our problems are our own'. I wanted for men to feel that these were their problems too, that these issues were shared.

But we did make some headway locally, even though feminists were generally not looked upon positively – and this included my parents as well.

Margherita Galati was 16 or 17 at the time, and has similar memories of what the club meant for her, and how the older generation tried to stop her from taking part:

My elder brother suggested I start going to Music and Culture because they used to show films there. And I must say, it was thanks to Peppino I began to understand the reality of the town I lived in and to keep my distance from certain kinds of people.

We used to get pressured at home by our families, though. They'd say to us: 'you shouldn't go there, it's a place of perdition. You'll end up being prostitutes, you'll totally lose your way.' My mother used to lose her temper and pull me by the hair, banging my head against the wall – so my reaction was to keep on going there.

The growth of a feminist group was something Peppino was very proud about. In fact, he used to boast to his male friends that feminists had knitted a jumper for him.

In any event Music and Culture filled a yawning gap for young people tired of traditional family life and the eternal immobility of peasant culture. Such was its success that the Communist Party, now worried about a sizeable young left-wing opposition that had rooted itself in the town, unsuccessfully tried to gain control over it.

The Impastatos: A Family at War

Peppino's activities ratcheted up the tension in the Impastato household. His mother Felicia recounts the reaction of his angry father: 'I wanted to run away ... when my husband rang the door bell I used to run into the bathroom. There were always arguments because they used to come and tell him: "hey, your son has just made a speech, he had a go at the Mafia".' Luigi used to tell his wife: '"he can talk about anything, all the other parties, the fascists ... but he absolutely can't talk about the Mafia" – you couldn't touch the Mafia, it was *untouchable*.' Felicia tried to hold Peppino back: 'I used to tell Peppino to watch what he was doing – "Be careful", and he used to answer – "people and kids need to be told what the Mafia is".' If the Mafia was meant to be untouchable, then Peppino was unstoppable.

Looking back many years later Peppino's mother recognised that the best thing she could have done was to leave her husband. Yet back in those days this was far easier said than done, particularly for a woman of her generation: 'Who would have helped me?' she wondered, rightly raising the prospect of being a social outcast if she left her husband. The cultural set-up back then was that as a mother and wife Felicia had duties on both levels, she belonged to others and could not make a decision independently of them, especially one that would destroy the conventional family structure.

Despite all of this, Felicia was a very modern woman. Another woman who was fast becoming a fixture in the household – Giovanni's girlfriend Felicetta – was surprised at the openness of this woman forty years her senior:

When I first started coming to this house what struck me was that she read a lot of newspapers – there were always five or six on the table – which Peppino had bought. Given that she was on her own a lot she would read them as well. Giovanni was off working with his father, whereas Peppino was upstairs studying. Then he would come downstairs and leave the papers on the table.

Felicia was old-fashioned and modern at the same time. I think she got a lot of this from Peppino, whereas Peppino got his character from her – strong and decisive. He also got his subtle irony from her too.

By now it wasn't just Peppino's newspaper articles and speeches that were annoying the Mafia. He would frequently make very precise accusations about the links between *Mafiosi* and local politicians – clearly somebody was giving him inside information. It's never been clear who passed these details over to him. Pino Vitale, another campaigner in the same group thinks: 'it could have been a cousin – Stefano Impastato – who was mayor for a while. He didn't agree with his other Christian Democrat councillors, so he might have had a reason to give him information. But Peppino never revealed who his informant was, because if it became known then the source would have dried up.' Another definite source were the anonymous letters he often received.

Much of this activity was often just background noise for Peppino's father. But, as Felicia says: 'Sometimes things were calm at home. But during election campaigns arguments used to break out.' Locally Peppino was growing in stature; some people might still disagree with him, but many others now listened to what he said. This was a worry for politicians concerned that their Mafia links might be made public. And all of this got back to her husband Luigi: 'As soon as he heard that Peppino and his friends were organising a meeting he got angry,' but this wasn't just because of what his eldest son was doing: 'he wanted Giovanni to keep his distance from Peppino. But I'd tell him: "Giovanni should go with this brother, he should be by his side." That's what I wanted.' Luigi wanted the opposite, for Peppino to work in his shop, alongside his brother Giovanni, in the hope of keeping him out of trouble – but Peppino wasn't interested.

Giovanni was starting to identify with his elder brother: 'We always felt that my father had made a choice to become a slave to the power of the Mafia – our choices were liberation and democracy.' But Peppino was far beyond Giovanni's position and this created problems between them, as he openly admits:

> I was younger and I was afraid. I didn't agree with his method of clashing with the Mafia head-on. But in some ways I was jealous of him, also because for good or bad all attention was focused on him. So automatically I was excluded, almost ignored, and this was a burden for me. We used to argue frequently, and sometimes we even came to blows.

Sometimes family tensions exploded in public, such as the evening that a new open-air pizzeria was opened at the side of the Impastato family shop, when a group of Peppino's friends decided to play some music to celebrate. One of them, Giovanni Riccobono, remembers: 'I was operating the lights. Something must have happened between him and Giovanni, because at a certain point Peppino starting grabbing bottles and throwing them in the bushes.' Salvo Vitale, who was playing bass guitar, adds, 'Then he stormed off in a foul mood. I never found out why.'

Not only was Giovanni trying to deal with an older and highly strung brother, but, as he said, there was also the fear that arose from his awareness of the Mafia's power: '*Mafiosi* used to go regularly to council meetings to check on what was happening. They would often go to Christian Democrat public meetings too.' Naturally they didn't take part in the debate, they just wanted everyone to see that they were there, keeping an eye on everyone. Because Giovanni wasn't rushing around writing leaflets, organising meetings and giving speeches, he had more time to observe what was going on. He was largely outside the intensely political atmosphere of Peppino's group, and perhaps he could gauge the opinions of ordinary local people better, who after all were his customers day after day at the family shop.

Giovanni used to see policemen and *Mafiosi*: 'walking down the street together as friends. They often went into a bar for a coffee together. There was a *carabiniere* colonel in Terrasini, Lombardo, who was always hanging around with them. You used to see this all over town, a very direct relationship between the Mafia and the police.' The strength of the Mafia doesn't just lie in their ability to kill people; if they can create a situation where they also control the police and politicians then people lose all hope in democracy and justice, and just become more and more scared.

Even though Felicia agreed with Peppino's stance, she was getting increasingly worried: 'I used to say to him – "you're a dead man. Don't keep making trouble." I often went upstairs to his room and jumbled everything up, creating a big mess.' All this tension even produced a chink of humanity in her husband, who told her: 'Get him to stop. Tell him to stop. He's digging his own grave, that's what he's doing.' He only said this to her alone, at night, so as not to lose face in front of his children. The possibility of actually losing his son had occurred to him, and for the first time he started to grapple with his conflicting loyalties towards his son and his Mafia friends.

For Felicia, her husband's shift made her blood run cold: 'at night in bed I'd grind everything over in my mind'. She obviously wasn't upset about her husband talking to her, searching to find a way for his son to reduce his 'exposure'. But what her husband had told her confirmed something that had been preying on her mind: 'That's how I knew they were talking about it' – 'it' being murdering Peppino.

Radio Aut

Unlike many other countries, setting up a radio station in Italy is fairly easy – access is not denied on the spurious grounds of a lack of waveband space, or the payment of expensive licence fees to the authorities. And back in the 1970s, in the last few years before television became the dominant media, young activists made ample use of 'free' radio stations. The first ever 'free' radio was set up by the civil rights campaigner Danilo Dolci in Partinico in March 1970, a man whose activities had impressed Peppino and others a few years earlier. This Radio of the New Resistance only lasted a couple of days before it was closed down by police, but the issues it brought out, the authorities' lack of support for people who had suffered in an earthquake in 1968, created a national debate.

Five years later another attempt was made, using Danilo Dolci's transmitter, but on this occasion Radio Free Wave lasted for several years. The driving force behind it was Gino Scasso, who had been at the centre of the 1968 student movement at Milan's Cattolica University, before moving back to his hometown of Partinico and being elected as a far left councillor in 1970. Perhaps one of the reasons it lasted so long, as he explains, was because: 'it wasn't just a militant radio station because we didn't have a group of activists prepared to dedicate themselves to that alone. So there were a lot of request shows and some serious music programmes that played jazz.' Scasso also remembers: 'Peppino used to come to the studio sometimes'; they had been at high school together in Partinico a few years earlier. Always open to new ideas, Peppino got involved: 'I can remember one particular story I followed with Peppino, a young woman from a very poor family, mentally disabled, who had been abducted from Cinisi station and raped.' The mushrooming of these revolutionary radio stations was so widespread that the transmitter that activists from Cinisi were to use came from a failed experiment that had only lasted a few months in the nearby town of Castellammare del Golfo.

1 Cinisi, showing the motorway, the main street (the Corso), the airport runway and the sea

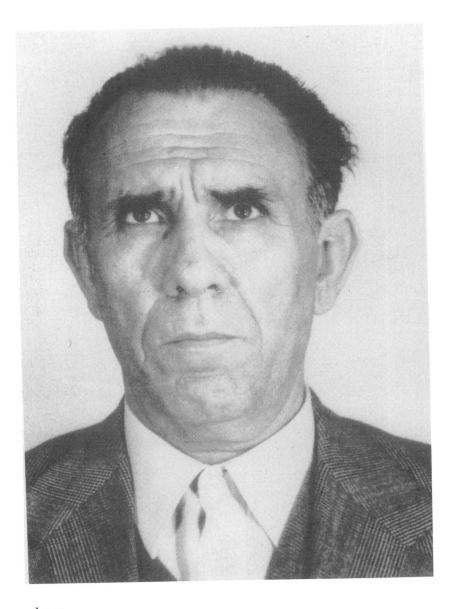

above
2 'Don Tano' – Gaetano Badalamenti

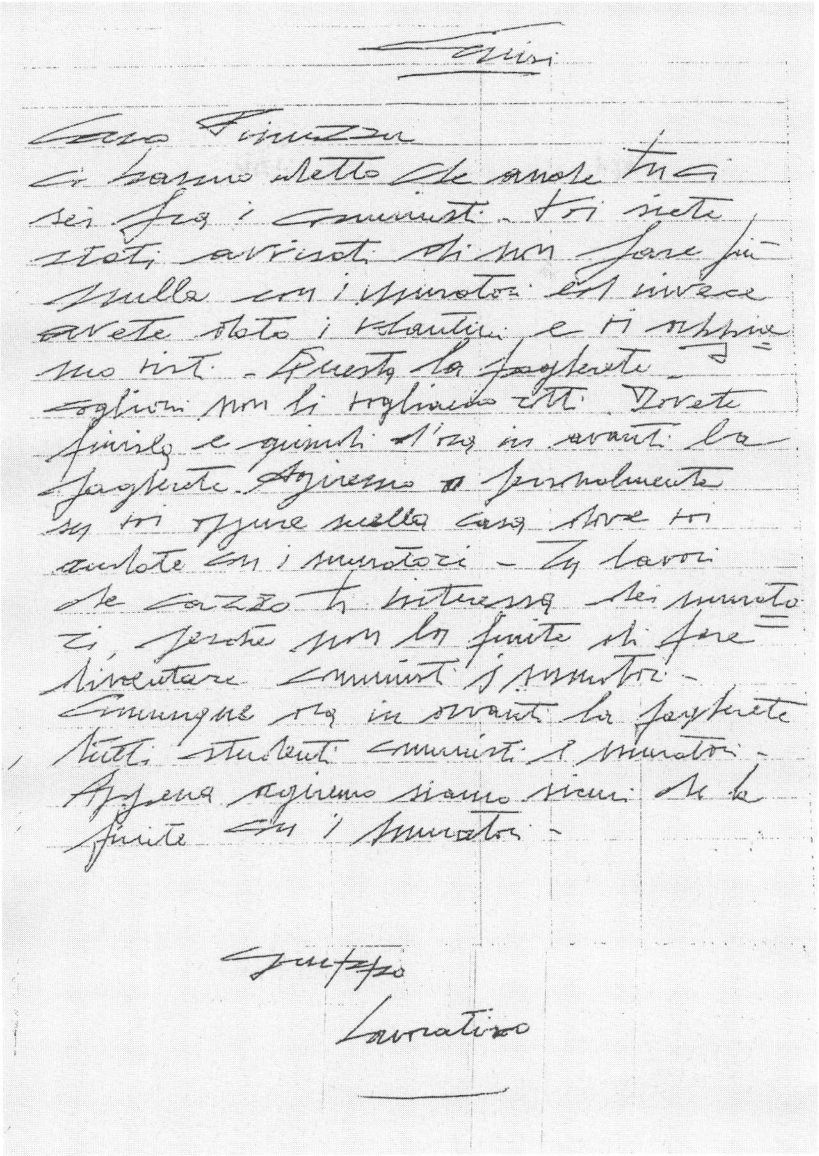

Cinisi

Caro Finazzo
ci hanno detto che ancora tu
sei fra i comunisti. Voi siete
stati avvisati di non fare più
nulla con i muratori e invece
avete fatto i volantini e vi abbia-
mo visti. Questa la pagherete.
sogliono non li togliamo tutti. Dovete
finirla e quindi d'ora in avanti la
pagherete. Agiremo o personalmente
su voi oppure nella casa dove voi
andate con i muratori. Tu lavori
del cazzo ti interessa dei muratori, perché non la finite di fare
diventare comunisti i muratori.
Comunque ora in avanti la pagherete
tutti studenti comunisti e muratori.
Appena agiremo siamo sicuri che la
finite con i muratori.

Gruppo
Lavoratori

above
6 Threatening letter sent to local activists (see page 93)

facing page
5 Peppino Impastato

7 A meeting of the Music and Culture group

8 Front blinds of the Impastato house

above
9 Giovanni
Impastato

right
10 A funeral in
Cinisi. From
left to right:
Felicetta Vitale,
Felicia Impastato,
Giovanni
Impastato and
aunt Fara

11 A house confiscated from the Badalamenti family, with Mount Pecoraro in the background

12 A funeral procession on Cinisi's main street

This was the background to Radio Aut being set up in a private house in the back streets of Terrasini. Broadcasting for several hours a day, the political input was strong but not overwhelming. Not only were there daily news bulletins with information from all over the world, but in September 1977 Peppino travelled as far as Bologna with bulky radio equipment to record debates and interviews at a three-day conference against state repression.

Peppino's main contribution was a show named *Crazy Wave*, which went out on Friday evenings, and was repeated on Sunday mornings. It was partly improvised, although a safety net of sound effects was always used. People would bring a bottle of wine, bread and olives, a record or two, and the microphones would be switched on. In many ways it was his crowning achievement – he was able to let rip with all his political passion and satirical imagination. Although he was a very private person, everybody recognised that when it came to talking about politics in public Peppino was a 'great communicator'. The recordings that have survived show that, considering they were complete amateurs operating with rudimentary equipment, the quality was very high.

The broadcasters self-mockingly defined it as a 'satirical-schizophrenic' show, and it is fair to say it was surreally political. By now Peppino was knocking at an open door: his political reputation as a straight shooter had already earned him large audiences when he gave speeches, and when *Crazy Wave* went out radio was still probably as popular as television in the homes of southern Italians. Many people would carry their transistor radios into bars, and groups would gather to enjoy the show. The powerful, meanwhile, would stay home to hide their embarrassment.

In order to avoid both legal problems and to amuse his audience, Peppino re-created Cinisi, its corrupt politicians and *Mafiosi* through the use of nicknames. The whole town was renamed 'Mafiopoli', and instead of using the real name of the town's main street, Corso Umberto, he changed it to 'Corso Luciano Leggio' – after one of the three top Mafia leaders of the time. Important local people were given nicknames, often relating to the American

Wild West. 'Geronimo' was in fact the Christian Democrat mayor Gero di Stefano, 'Joe the Hod Carrier' was the Mafia building contractor Giuseppe Finazzo, Badalamenti's deputy Vito Palazzolo became Cinisi council's 'Minister for Foreign Affairs' due to his frequent trips to the US – a description many people would have presumed referred to his involvement in international drug trafficking. Peppino's favourite target was Don Tano Badalamenti, whom he sometimes called a 'pale-face', and here some explanation of Italian is necessary to understand the Wild West allusion. The leader of the Oglala Sioux, Sitting Bull is translated into Italian as 'Toro seduto' – so Tano Badalamenti became Tano Seduto.

The force of these programmes went far beyond clever puns and nicknames; they were a political podium from which Peppino and others used one of the most formidable weapons that can weaken the powerful – satire.

The following monologue not only attacks another sacred cow – the Church – it also attacks the Christian Democrats, while all the time making sarcastic remarks about Badalamenti. The timing of this broadcast, just two weeks before a council election, also increased its effect:

> . . . yes, yes, they're all going to pray, they're praying the elections go well and that all the faithful convert to the Christian Democrats. They're always praying: *in the name of the Father the Son and the Holy Ghost, in Earth as it be in Heaven* – but look how many nuns there are!!! – a hell of a lot of nuns, who are all with us. And then, and then, and then there are some friends, who are praying for them as well: *our Father, here as thou art in Heaven*, and they're all praying for a CD victory, Don Tano, Don Tano, who is a man of great faith, of immense faith, a man who deeply believes in God and in eternal peace, Don Tano, a man who has given two million lire to celebrate our patron saint, two million, he paid for the whole celebration. Don Tano, who has never been a bad Christian but always a devout Christian, Don Tano, Don Tano is praying . . . (soundtrack from a Western film, gunshots).

Don Tano is praying for a Christian Democrat victory, so that the CD gets in the best position, so that everybody bends over and offers their arses ... 'dear brethren, give us some help'... Don Tano Seduto is overcome, at the moment he is paying penance for all the sins he has committed so that the brethren of Mafiopoli and the holy CD forgive him ... 'My dear brethren, I have cleansed myself, now I am pure, my act of penance is a sign that I have returned to the flock, that I am praying for you, that my sacrifices have been for you. I beseech you in the name of my earlier teachings' (gunshots) – vote Christian Democrat.

An Expert in Heroin Trafficking and Shotguns

These radio shows were very popular in town, and they must have been very enjoyable to make. But Peppino and others didn't forget that they were still engaged in a deadly serious campaign to change Cinisi from head to foot.

The central political problem they had campaigned against for a decade was still there: a system of power formally dominated by the Christian Democrats, but in which the Mafia had a strong influence. Jets now screamed overhead in the lower areas of Cinisi and heavy traffic was still clogging up some streets as construction work for the new motorway had not yet finished. Following the worldwide success of *The Godfather* there was even an obscene element of 'Mafia tourism', mainly involving British visitors. Once a week a coach would leave a resort along the coast and climb up into the mountains behind Cinisi on a day trip. It cost 2,500 lire to visit 'The Godfather' and receive a kiss on the cheek and a glass of wine. However, there wasn't much play-acting going on: Pietro 'The Damned' Palazzolo – the human 'tourist attraction' in question – had recently been serving a life sentence for no less than 13 murders. He was a typical specimen also in his apparent deep sense of respect towards others. Margherita Galati met him several times because at the time she was a friend of his granddaughter:

'he was a real gentleman, with a real sense of reverence towards the family and towards women'. While all of this was simply in bad taste, what was truly scandalous was that Cinisi council had spent a huge amount building a road that led to virtually Palazzolo's house alone.

What perhaps made Peppino and others angrier more than anything else was that the Communist Party was slowly but surely sliding into this swamp. This was the background to a meeting held one day in April 1977, when the group argued strongly over the text of a leaflet. Many said it was over the top, but in the end it was printed and they allowed Peppino to distribute it. It contains all the anger, frustration and sense of betrayal they felt towards the Communist Party, but Peppino distributed it virtually on his own. As regards both the Christian Democrats and the Mafia, they had never gone this far before:

> Following the passing of the council budget, due to the votes of the Communists, Socialists, Liberals and fascists, which will allow Christian Democrat DICKHEADS to manage the town's affairs for a long period, the planning committee has practically approved an application to build a five-storey building. It was presented by the notorious Giuseppe Finazzo, 'hod carrier' of Gaetano Badalamenti, a pale-face expert in heroin trafficking and shotguns . . .
>
> First of all we accuse the Christian Democrats of being enslaved to the Mafia, given that they have allowed our whole area to be devastated in recent years, something which has been led by the Badalamenti gang, who have made sizeable profits which they have then recycled into other 'business'.
>
> We demand that the Communist and Socialist parties publicly account for their political behaviour over the last few years . . .
>
> ONCE AGAIN, WE DEMAND THESE SO-CALLED LEFT-WING PARTIES ACT RESPONSIBILY, BOTH POLITICALLY AND SOCIALLY: you're either with the Mafia and the Christian Democrats or you're against them.
>
> In any event, we've got sufficient evidence to unmask you once and for all.

A few days later there was a knock on the door of the Impastatos' house on the Corso. It was a well-known Badalamenti henchman, who had something to say to Luigi Impastato.

This had never happened before: Luigi had always made arrangements and gone to meetings of his own accord, his family never knew precisely when he was seeing his Mafia friends. The Mafia is always very careful and precise about how it communicates, and it often does so by sending unspoken messages. Don Tano's open message, to all those who heard it – or who would hear about it – was that he wanted to meet Peppino's father right away.

Accidental Death of a *Mafioso*?

Felicia recounts what happened a few days after that knock on the door:

> I had invited my daughter-in-law to lunch. When we had stopped eating he took down his suitcases and said to me: 'Get my things ready because I'm going away.' 'And why are you leaving?' I asked him. 'I'm going away until things quieten down' he replied. But what did that mean?
>
> 'I can't stay inside this house any longer, I'm ashamed!' 'What is there to be ashamed about? It's not as if your boys have stolen or killed, or run around with bad women. What are you ashamed of?' He answered: 'I can't stay here any more, I've got to leave . . . I'll come back when things have been sorted out, otherwise I'll never come back.'

This is the typical brusque manner of a traditional patriarch – no explanation, no discussion, just action. Amazed by his behaviour, his daughter-in-law Felicetta Vitale attacked him too: 'But what do you mean? You're acting like a baby.'

Luigi Impastato's weakness was clear for all to see. His leaving must have had something to do with his meeting with Badalamenti; whatever he was doing now was happening because he had been told to do it. He didn't want to discuss things with his family and explain why he was taking such drastic action. So he just doggedly stuck to his guns: 'I'm going, and if anybody asks for me, say that I'm going for work.'

Felicia was exasperated: 'I responded by saying I didn't want to know a thing, and that all he should do was leave.' And with that he was gone. On the short drive to the airport, Luigi told a relative: 'I'll come back when things are sorted out. Look out for Giovanni though – because my other son is a lost cause.'

That was it. Nobody even knew where he had gone, and as to why he had gone – all they knew was that 'things had to be sorted out'.

A whole series of questions arose in the minds of those he had left behind: what was it that needed sorting out? Was it Peppino? Why did Luigi have to leave so that things could get sorted out? Should Peppino change his behaviour? Should the family send some kind of message to Badalamenti? Should they just carry on as before and wait for Luigi to come back? None of these questions had simple or easy answers.

As Felicia recounts, her eldest son did not seem prepared to change tack in the face of his father's sudden disappearance: 'When my husband went to America, the person who was struck the most was Peppino. He said, "He's gone to America to let me be killed, who cares?"' His mother, though, was very worried, so she asked Peppino: 'Why don't you carry a gun?' This wasn't such an unusual question to ask, hunting has always been popular in Italy and these small Sicilian towns had always been awash with guns.

Maybe five years earlier Peppino might have responded differently, but the political climate had changed dramatically over the last couple of years. On the mainland a left-wing terrorist group called the Red Brigades had launched a spectacular series of kneecappings, bank robberies, and lately political assassinations. Although they called themselves communists, they were a very elitist group: all their supporters had to do was to just sit at home and watch – the communism they apparently wanted to create would be the work of a few hundred terrorists. Not only was their strategy doomed to failure; when the Red Brigades attacked the establishment it gave the Christian Democrats and the police a stick they could beat radicals such as Peppino with. If democratic revolutionaries such as Peppino – whose concept of communism came through mass action – could somehow be associated with the Red Brigades, he and others like him could be criminalised and therefore removed as a serious force of opposition. This was the thinking behind Peppino's answer to his mother: 'If I were to carry a gun, given that the police are in agreement with the Mafia, they'd take me in as an armed terrorist.'

Meanwhile, Luigi Impastato had caught a flight to America.

First he went to New Orleans and stayed with the children of his brother, 'Leadspitter' Impastato. Then he went to stay with other relatives near Los Angeles, but the fact that he arrived without warning them was proof of his confused state of mind. Yet the change did him good. He was far away from Cinisi, totally separated from his hometown. Trips across the Atlantic were very expensive, as were transatlantic phone calls, so he had no contact with Cinisi. Not only was he more relaxed, but in the US he had no 'face' to lose, he could say what he thought and talk far more freely than he could with his wife and sons.

So he started to open up a bit, and told his relatives that Peppino: 'talked an awful lot'. But he also uttered a key phrase: 'I've told them – they'll have to kill me first before they kill Peppino'. He admitted to his relatives across the Atlantic what he had never told his family in Cinisi: that his Mafia friends had discussed killing Peppino. Once again, given that he no longer felt he had to act like an alpha male, he started to talk about his feelings. Despite all his blunt arguments, insults and brutality, he wanted to defend his son and protect him – something he would never admit to back home.

Many things still weren't clear, though: what did the Cinisi Mafia think of his attitude? Perhaps they respected traditional family loyalty and would let things lie. But what if Peppino carried on – could there be a breaking point? And how serious was Luigi's threat to defend his son at all costs?

None of these conversations filtered back to his family. After about a week they did find out where he was, yet they still didn't know why he was there. There were a couple of theories being tossed around by the family: firstly that it was just a vindictive act, aimed at punishing them by making them worry and suffer; the second idea was that he had left Cinisi to give the Mafia an opportunity to kill Peppino. It obviously wasn't the latter, because when Luigi came back after a month all of his family were still doing very much the same things. Once again, he told them nothing. Did the fact he was now back meant that whatever had driven him away had been 'sorted out'? Nevertheless his wife remembers: 'When he got back from America he seemed better'.

Maybe what had been sorted out was in Luigi's mind; perhaps he had decided to come off the fence and defend his son. Soon after his return, his brother 'Leadspitter' Impastato told another relative: 'A few days ago my brother Luigi almost had a go at me. He's gone mad, he doesn't think straight. He agrees with everything his wife says.' Not only was this a terrible situation for a male chauvinist to witness, but once again it suggests that Luigi Impastato was not prepared to stand by and let his son be murdered.

Soon after his return the family went out to eat, as Felicia recalls:

> We were at the pizzeria one evening in September. It was near closing time as the waiters were packing things away, and my husband said, 'I'll go on ahead.' So I got into the car with my daughter-in-law, but when we got home there was nobody in. We retraced our steps and she saw him lying on the ground, dead.

A car had stopped nearby. Afterwards the driver said she had never seen anybody, but had felt the car drive over something on the road.

Luigi Impastato was dead – but who had killed him – the driver or somebody else? It is perfectly possible that it was an accident, after all, the bumper had been damaged. On the other hand, the Mafia could well have had an interest in getting rid of him.

As with any family, the death of the father obliged those left to take stock. This was one of Giovanni's thoughts: 'When my father died I felt a huge sense of liberation inside me – "at last I'm free", I said to myself. On the other hand, I did feel a lot of pain because the person who had brought me into the world had died.' But his mother was worried about her other son: 'As soon as my husband had his accident I immediately thought, "my son's already dead".'

Despite any suspicions the family might have had, and despite Peppino's activities, Badalamenti visited Felicia to pay his condolences: 'he was here in front of me, he was paying his respects. I would have liked to throw him out but I didn't, I was worried about Peppino. We really were on our own.' Whether they were behind Luigi's death or not, the Mafia quickly discovered that Peppino had not changed his attitude. All the top *Mafiosi* turned out for the funeral, but at the cemetery Peppino stood with his arms folded across his chest when they walked up to him to offer him their condolences – not even with his father's death would Peppino show Mafia bosses any respect and shake their hands.

Meanwhile, Felicia had managed to get Peppino to respond to their changed situation: 'He went to Milan for a month and then he came back. He was meant to go to America, my cousin was waiting for him and he had agreed to go. But in the meantime the elections were announced and he decided to stand.'

11

The Last Crazy Wave

A new national organisation came into being in 1977 – Proletarian Democracy – which contained within it most of the various strands of the small revolutionary parties that had folded over the previous two years. In Partinico, Gino Scasso signed his party card and recounts what happened next:

> When Peppino told me he was prepared to stand as a Proletarian Democracy candidate, I organised a meeting at Radio Aut between him, myself and the only representative we had within national institutions at that time, a senator from Arezzo, Dante Rossi. As a newly formed party we were willing to support Peppino, but the senator imposed one condition: 'you're going to have to make it very clear you have nothing to do with the Red Brigades'.

It might seem strange for the senator to make such a big fuss about this, particularly when there had been no left-wing terrorist actions in Sicily. The problem was that the media and some political parties would sometimes use a few actions taking place at the other end of Italy to suggest there was an imminent threat of terrorism in Sicily. Public opinion would become worried, and politically it would become easier to isolate and damage people who criticised the government's policies.

One instructive example had occurred two years before Peppino decided to stand at Alcamo Marina, just a few miles away from Cinisi, when two policemen were murdered in cold blood in their barracks. Even the most inexperienced police officer knew that Alcamo, Cinisi and Partinico were towns full of powerful Mafia gangs dealing in drugs, extortion rackets, building speculation, kidnappings, illegal production of wine and the procurement of public sector contracts. These were also areas where there had been no left-wing terrorist actions whatsoever.

Yet, following these murders, the police raided hundreds of houses belonging to members of the Communist Party and the revolutionary left, including five in Cinisi, while *Mafiosi* houses were left untouched. The two people later convicted of the murders had nothing to do with the Red Brigades.

This was part of the 'strategy of tension', a conspiracy between elements of the police, the secret services and the Christian Democrats to accuse the far left of any act of violence that took place in the country. The underlying reason for this strategy was that in recent years the left had been growing electorally and, equally, trade unions had become strong. Even in a small town such as Cinisi ordinary people had the confidence to stand up and show the power their jobs gave them. As Pino Vitale remembers:

> Myself and Rosario Rappa were charged following a dispute in 1977. The situation was that we were electricians who would pass from one contractor to another, but the work we did was always the same – electrical maintenance at the airport. Because a new contractor didn't want to take us on a dispute developed, and I can remember writing a leaflet with Peppino. I remember once we switched the airport lights off for a whole night and several flights were cancelled. It was treated so seriously we were even called to a meeting at the Ministry of Transport in Rome.

Despite the risk of other parties playing the 'terrorist card', and the fact that Peppino made no secret of his belief in revolution, many moderate people in Cinisi had come to respect Peppino. He had received a significant number of votes when he stood as a candidate for regional government a few years earlier, and his speeches were always attended by large crowds. Furthermore, there was a new wave of young voters, given that the minimum voting age in council elections had been reduced from 21 to 18 in 1975. In other words, it certainly wasn't beyond the bounds of possibility that he would be elected as a councillor. His chances of getting elected were probably high because he promised to reveal even more of the shady dealings going on between the local council and Mafia bosses. Not only was there no other candidate prepared to stand on such a platform, but Peppino already had a record that was second to none in exposing corruption and collusion.

All this was swirling around a recently widowed woman in her 60s, his mother Felicia: 'I lived through a terrible period. I used to wake up at night and go and check that Giovanni was there . . .'; she was worried about Giovanni because of Peppino:

> I used to talk about the Mafia with Peppino. I told him I hated the Mafia as well, we're decent people, but he didn't listen. I used to say to him: 'snuffing out a candle is nothing to them, it doesn't take long to dig a grave because they're animals.' Well really they're worse – at least you can reason with some animals, but with them it's impossible. They're wild animals. The Mafia won't listen to people.

During the election campaign another close relative tried to dissuade Peppino too:

> I really begged him. I remember we were in the kitchen, and I told him: 'Look, Peppino, this is a terrible period. These people are killing each other as well, nowadays they've got no respect for anyone. Why don't you stop

what you're doing – why don't you go to Bologna?' – I said that because I knew he had friends there. 'You could build a political organisation there, just as you want, and once it's grown you could come back to Sicily.' But I was just clutching at straws. He turned round, raising one of the fingers of his hand, and he said: 'They can all dance on this.'

Deep down, Peppino was paying a heavy price for his commitment. There was no end of ways in which the Mafia could try to 'get' to him, so perhaps the only way to survive was absolute self-control. Graziella Iacopelli, then a teenager, who knew him slightly remembers, 'Peppino wasn't the kind of person who easily let himself go.' She recalls, 'he always used to dress in black', and she used to see him walking along the Corso, but in such a way that you could see his nervous energy; he would bob and weave as he walked almost like a boxer does in the ring. Another teenager at the time, Margherita Galati, says: 'He always used to bite his nails.' This was perhaps one of the few slight chinks in his armour, otherwise: 'Peppino was very withdrawn. And sometimes his loneliness really touched me.'

The amateur actor Gaspare Cucinella knew him better because in this period he was working closely with Peppino on the *Crazy Wave* programme for Radio Aut:

> He always had his mind elsewhere, preoccupied with something or other. He was never calm, and that's why his life in this dirty filthy town was so difficult . . .
>
> He was alone, totally alone . . .
>
> Peppino worked himself too hard. Inside, he was falling to bits. He was on his own – totally – and this loneliness made him very sad. Physically he had become very weak, he hardly ate anything, sometimes he was put on an intravenous drip to pick himself up.

Near the end of election campaign Cucinella bumped into Peppino and found him tired and disappointed, so 'I suggested that he come and stay at my house for a couple of weeks, to get away from such a worrying environment. He said that he couldn't, he had to see the election campaign through, and that in any case there was no need to worry.'

Soon after the calling of council elections something had happened that raised the political temperature even further: former Prime Minister Aldo Moro was kidnapped in Rome by the Red Brigades. It was a brutally efficient action: five bodyguards were killed, and the Christian Democrats' most senior statesman was now in a self-styled 'people's prison' facing a 'trial', at the end of which nearly everybody expected him to be sentenced to death. At the same time, the Red Brigades demanded the opening of negotiations for the release of some of their members held in prison.

To cynical Christian Democrats this was a gift – after all, if politicians were prepared to do deals with *Mafiosi* then it was clear they had very little morals. First of all, for as long as Moro was held they could milk public sympathy because their leader was facing execution by terrorists. Secondly, and this went on for much of the 1970s, right-wing politicians and their friends in the media could insinuate that the Communist Party was in sympathy with 'the Reds'.

Rather than stressing their total lack of any links with terrorism, and exposing the Christian Democrats' cynical exploitation of their leader's personal nightmare, the Communists dutifully played the role assigned to them: a week before the election a local Communist MP gave a speech in Cinisi in which he attacked 'the mummy's boys, the dangerous accomplices of terrorists'. The end result that was hoped for was that all opposition to the Christian Democrats would cease, given the need – in the Communist Party's eyes – for 'national unity' to face 'the terrorist threat'.

Not for the first time, Peppino wrote on behalf of Proletarian Democracy a condemnation of the Red Brigades, which he defined as:

> The party of death, of fear, of expropriation of mass struggle. Moro murdered would reinforce this state; the

government would enjoy the consensus it has so cynically sought by refusing to negotiate and ratcheting up the strongest threat possible to national security ... Until the last possible moment we will repeat our proposal to negotiate. It isn't only Moro's life that is at stake: a dramatic situation of gang warfare must be avoided in our country. Mass struggles must become the driving force of social transformation.

In the midst of this hostage crisis that was followed throughout the world, Peppino and others didn't forget about their own 'enemy within', the Mafia. They mounted a photographic exhibition along the Corso – dozens of panels roughly two feet by four feet. Called 'Exhibition About our Territory', it illustrated and explained in great detail the local council's corruption and collusion with the Mafia. Displayed as it was on the main street, the whole town could not avoid seeing in great detail the dirty linen of local politicians being washed in public.

It was clear that these 'mummy's boys, the dangerous accomplices of terrorists' were a force to be reckoned with. Otherwise why, three weeks before polling day, was sugar poured into the petrol tank of Peppino's car, with which he planned to drive around with a loudspeaker making electoral announcements? After all, what would be the point in damaging the activities of a candidate who stood no chance?

The strength of the election campaign could be seen when Peppino gave his final speech on the Corso. Even though it was raining there were hundreds of people, perhaps close to a thousand. This speech was being held at the same time as one by Piersanti Mattarella, president of the Sicilian Christian Democrats (who would be murdered by the Mafia two years later), who was due to speak in the square in front of the council building. Shortly before Mattarella began speaking, two people went up the Corso and saw there were just a few dozen people getting ready to hear Sicily's most powerful politician. Margherita Galati's recollections end with perhaps a bit of an understatement:

'When Peppino gave his final campaign speech it was packed, and he was very explicit about naming names. He had created widespread consensus and this worried certain people.'

Petty censorship also illustrated the fear his candidacy had created. During the campaign Peppino gave an interview to a local radio station in Terrasini, but they bleeped out the word 'Mafia' every time he used the expression 'Christian Democracy is Mafia'. Despite all these difficulties at least Peppino's campaign had Radio Aut, and they made full use of it. In such a tense period, Felicia remembers: 'I didn't have the courage to listen to it. Sometimes Giovanni switched it on and I told him: 'For the love of God, switch it off'.' In their last broadcast before election day, Peppino and the rest showed that they would not stop attacking the Mafia. It was also clear, once again, that they knew all the council's dirty secrets:

> [WHISPERED]
> 1st voice: Ssshhh! Quiet! The electoral rules committee is meeting in Mafiopoli. They're dividing up the cake.
> 2nd voice: Ah the cake – and there's a bit for everyone.
> 1st voice: No, there's not! They're only dividing it up amongst themselves. And they're dividing up the returning officers.
> 2nd voice: Shit! What's it all mean?
> 1st voice: They get paid – 40,000 lire each.
> 2nd voice: They're all going bla-bla-bla. What's it mean?
> 1st voice: They're dividing up the returning officers on the basis of how many votes every party is expected to get. And it seems the party of the advanced left [the Communist Party] took part in this secret meeting – just like the ones held by the Red Brigades. And now we can bring you the official results of who the returning officers will be.
> 2nd voice: Christian Democrats – 27, with nine to the advanced left. We can now bring you the latest

news: the Christian Democrats have told Don Tano they're willing to give him all 27 returning officers, but we don't know whether Don Tano Seduto has accepted their offer (cow noises).

12

And the Windows Stayed Shut

Anatomy of Human Destructiveness

Three nights after this radio broadcast about election irregularities, Fara Bartolotta came back home after midnight. She shared her house, just outside Cinisi station, with her nephew Peppino. She didn't look in his room because Peppino often came home late as well, so she went straight to bed.

An hour later the driver of the midnight train from Palermo stopped his locomotive out near the airport. He climbed down and saw the line was twisted and broken, but luckily the train hadn't jumped the tracks. He started to search in the dark; Peppino's car was parked nearby. It quickly became clear to him a bomb had gone off. Several sticks of dynamite had exploded, and human remains were scattered over a wide area.

Peppino's Aunt Fara got up early the next morning, about 5.30am, and noticed that he had not come back home. Worried by something so unusual, she rushed off to the house of her sister, Felicia.

Back at the railway lines, the human remains strewn around the railway tracks were identified as belonging to Peppino, dead at just 30 years old. *Ammazzarono*. At around 7am a separate police squad was sent to Aunt Fara's house. Not finding her there, they went on to her sister's house – a total of four vans went to his mother's house. Fara was taken back to search the house where Peppino lived. Like any political activist Peppino had lots of books, leaflets and notes scattered around his room.

One of the books they impounded had now taken on a lot of symbolic importance: *Anatomy of Human Destructiveness* was written by the German psychoanalyst Erich Fromm, a very popular writer among left-wingers in the 1960s. Fromm started from the fact that humans are the only species that inflicts pain and torture on others, the only animal that is violent when there is no threat, and tried to understand why. He concluded that this violence generally reached excessive levels only in the industrial era; human aggression is the inevitable outcome of a social system that seems actively designed to suppress positive outlets such as love and compassion, and to embed individuals as a cog in a machine.

The police, meanwhile, finished their search and left at about 8am. Back out near the airport, the police were getting ready to evacuate the site, even though they had received the first call about the incident just over four hours earlier. The remains of Peppino's body had been collected very hurriedly, and the track was repaired immediately. With hindsight, such eagerness to lose vital evidence was odd to say the least – after all, somebody had just been blown to bits for reasons that weren't immediately clear.

One piece of vital evidence was found, but it remained overlooked for many years. The council gravedigger who had been asked by the police to collect Peppino's remains had called them over to a small barn very near the explosion. Inside there were fresh bloodstains on two stones, and a trail of blood on the floor heading towards the door. The obvious presumption was that Peppino was wounded or killed inside, and then dragged out, therefore he couldn't have ignited any sticks of dynamite a hundred metres away on the railway tracks.

At around this time, 8am, Peppino's friends were arriving because they had heard what had happened. As soon as they approached the area a police superintendent saw them and said 'give me your details'. Once he had written them down in a little notebook he curtly told them: 'Go to the police station, we want to question you'. A line of police officers stopped them from walking onto the railway tracks, yet behind that line they could see ordinary people, people they knew from Cinisi, wandering about and satisfying their curiosity. This was the first of many negative signals from the police.

At around the same time in Partinico Gino Scasso was woken up and heard the word used so often in Cinisi: '*ammazzarono*'. 'Who?' 'Peppino'.

Although he speaks very slowly, and some people would call him dopey, the first thing Scasso did was to go to the Proletarian Democracy branch and burn all records of party membership. The man who had been killed had been standing as a Proletarian Democracy councillor, and the man burning party records was already a councillor for the same party in the next town. What was the connection between the dead man and the burning of party records? There was none, of course, but as Scasso explains: 'I knew immediately what kind of climate would be created, I knew immediately in which direction the police would take their investigations.'

Back in Cinisi, when some of Peppino's friends arrived at the police station for questioning, they noticed Peppino's car was already parked outside – a police officer must have driven it there. Anybody could touch it, adding new fingerprints or rubbing out others. The direction in which the police were taking the investigation became clear once the questioning began. Peppino's brother Giovanni endured a five-hour session that morning. They told him that his brother had 'died on the job', in the sense that he was a terrorist who was preparing a bomb. The statement Giovanni signed at midday revealed the kind of questions the police were asking: 'I have never seen my brother handling dynamite or other terrorist weaponry. He was against terrorism, practically everyone knows this. Until I see conflicting ballistic evidence I am convinced my brother was deliberately killed, and that those responsible wanted to make his death look like an accident which occurred when he was preparing a terrorist attack.'

Giovanni's girlfriend Felicetta also endured a long session. What she said in her statement at 2.30pm revealed a second line of police inquiry: 'it does not seem possible to me that he committed suicide; neither do I believe him capable of carrying out a terrorist attack.' Further on she added: 'I do not have strong arguments to back up what I have said above. I can say that he was against acts of violence.'

Naturally these young people were shocked and devastated by Peppino's death. Furthermore, they must have been deeply confused and disturbed by what the police were making them talk about. But despite the formal language of police statements, the words 'I do not have strong arguments to back up what I have said' show the kind of pressure they were being put under.

Years later another young man questioned that day, Giovanni Riccobono, explained in a hearing of the parliamentary Anti-Mafia Commission how they were treated:

> 'Following his death investigators took me and other friends of Peppino to the police station, where we were all harassed and treated like terrorists.' Asked to explain the content of that phrase further, he added: 'I used the term "harassed" because they kept on asking the same question: "Why were you organising a bombing?" We were supposed to answer that we were preparing a bomb, or that as we were placing it things went wrong and Peppino was killed. This is what I meant. We were asked the same question over and over again.'...
> 'From the very beginning we got the feeling they weren't interested in the truth. We all noticed that immediately. I repeat: they didn't ask us about anything else, all they said was that we were bombers.'... 'I, along with all the

others, made it clear that Peppino had written leaflets and
made speeches against the Mafia. In different ways, we
were all asking the police to investigate in that direction.'

By 8pm that evening three police officers in Cinisi signed
a document defining the explosion thus: 'such a criminal
action was presumably intended to cause a train crash'.
Other lines of inquiry were being ruled out, it was all as
easy as ABC – the officers were called Abramo, Buono and
Canale.

Aside from 'helping police with their inquiries', Peppino's
friends were facing their first big test without him: how to
respond publicly to his death, and their reaction had to be
immediate, his funeral would certainly not past unnoticed.
They decided to print a large poster and put it up in the
town, but they could get nobody in Cinisi to print it. Gino
Scasso recalls some of them arriving in Partinico: 'they
looked like they'd taken a real hammering'. Nobody in
Partinico would print it either, so they had to drive over to
a third town, Alcamo, where they finally found someone
prepared to do the work.

The explanation given in the poster for Peppino's death
was totally different to the one given by the police:

> Peppino Impastato has been murdered. His long activity
> as a revolutionary activist has been used by his murderers
> and 'the forces of law and order' to create the ridiculous
> notion of a terrorist attack. This is a lie! This murder has
> a very obvious explanation: MAFIA. As we gather together
> round Peppino's twisted body we make one single promise
> – to carry on the fight against his murderers. *Proletarian
> Democracy.*

The following day the main local investigator, Major Antonino
Subranni, continued in the same vein as his colleagues. He
entitled his report: 'Death of Peppino Impastato . . . due to a
terrorist attack carried out by himself'. In the main text he
spoke of Impastato: 'planning and carrying out an attack on
the railway line with dynamite, so as to link his death with
such a remarkable event'.

So according to the police Peppino had a death wish, but what was this 'remarkable event'? About 12 hours after the discovery of his mutilated body, Aldo Moro's body was found in the boot of a car in central Rome – the Red Brigades had killed him with 11 bullets fired at point-blank range. For 55 days the Italian police had failed to find him; the whole country and much of the world were talking about nothing but Italy's left-wing terrorists. The idea that Peppino had decided to blow himself up several hours before the 'remarkable event' of Moro's death obviously suggested that he was in direct contact with the Red Brigades' leadership.

Peppino's Funeral

Peppino's funeral would be a testing ground. His fellow comrades wanted it to be big, and to accuse those they viewed as being responsible for his death – the Mafia. The Mafia would have preferred no funeral at all, or if it went ahead they wanted it to be small; the smaller it was the clearer it would be to the town that Peppino was isolated, that the man who had exposed and irritated them intensely for more than ten years had no real support. The unstated views of senior policemen and Christian Democrats were probably quite similar to those of the Mafia. The Communist Party was deeply embarrassed, but more of that later.

The key response, the 'detonator' for good or bad, had to come from his family.

His mother remembers it as a turning point: 'My relatives didn't want it to take place, at that point there still hadn't been a definitive breakdown.' One of them, 80-year-old Nick 'Killer' Impastato, warned her in typical Mafia language: 'Be careful, for Giovanni's sake'. On one level he was expressing natural family concern for her one remaining son, but on another he was indirectly warning her that one day Giovanni could suffer the same fate.

Another notorious *Mafioso*, 'Leadspitter' Impastato – Felicia's brother-in-law – came to the funeral as well, along with his sons. But the local *Mafiosi* were to be deeply disappointed. Felicia remembers 'Leadspitter':

sat on a corner, and then my niece Maria came up in a big rush and says, 'Ah, Felicia, come here, look, there are loads of people – and look, even more people are gathering!' He went as white as a sheet, 'They're going to give me a hiding'. He was terrified, and asked for a glass of water because he looked as though he was going to die.

For a town of around eight to ten thousand people, Peppino's funeral was a huge procession, probably over a thousand people. Many mourners were young rather than old, and although people wore black there were political banners, one of which read: 'Peppino – murdered by the Christian Democrat Mafia'. It looked as if the Mafia hadn't got their way.

One image of that grey and overcast day still stands out. As the cortege set off, Giovanni suddenly raised his clenched fist high above the heads of mourners, giving the traditional Communist salute. It was the first sign that the Impastato family – Giovanni and his mother – were going to follow in Peppino's footsteps.

But as the angry march went down the Corso the windows of the houses stayed shut, the blinds of shops were not drawn down as the coffin passed. Most of the mourners were from outside Cinisi; the town as a whole had not shown its support. At the cemetery many of Peppino's comrades sang revolutionary songs over his grave, but it wasn't only these young radicals who disagreed with the police about how he had died. On the evening of his death Peppino had been due to meet his 50-year-old cousin who had just flown in from the US. She later recalled to investigators what people were saying: 'at the funeral all his relatives and many other people all mentioned the name of Don Tano Badalamenti, giving one single explanation – Peppino Impastato had been killed by the Mafia.'

Many people then marched back to the town square, where a rally was held. On their way up the Corso, some of Peppino's friends and comrades gathered in front of Badalamenti's house and shouted 'butcher'. Others threw stones at the windows of the Christian Democrats' local party branch. These were acts of courage and anger, but it soon became clear that they were isolated acts. As far as local people were concerned such actions created the same kind of echo a pin makes when it falls to the floor of a soundproofed room.

The following day Proletarian Democracy, the party for which Peppino had been a candidate, held its final rally, which had been organised long before; it was just three days before the local council election. Just as Giovanni's clenched fist salute illustrated that the driving force of Peppino's life would be defended, some of the people speaking at that rally represented the handing over of another baton in this fight against the Mafia – from Cinisi to Palermo. One of the speakers, Umberto Santino, was born just before the Second World War, and like many people born around this time he is very short, due to the acute hunger of the period. He has the look of an accountant about him but his ideas were unlike those of a stereotypical accountant – like Peppino he was a revolutionary Marxist.

One reason Santino was asked to speak was because people knew he had a lot of experience, given that he had already been deeply involved in far left activity throughout Sicily for several years. Another reason was that the year before he had created a research centre in Palermo on the Mafia, as he explains: 'When I founded the Centre, the Mafia was viewed as a phenomenon destined to disappear; so that's why I decided to found a research centre dedicated to analysing the Mafia and how it was changing.'

As regards his speech at the rally: 'I got up on this tiny little stage that had been built on the Corso, in front of the Christian Democrat offices, and I noticed that up and down the street virtually all the windows were shut.' But as ever on these occasions, there were many more people eagerly listening behind the blinds of closed windows. Just as with Peppino's radio shows, there was a passive audience listening to an anti-Mafia message. And the whole purpose of Peppino's life was to turn that passive sympathy into open opposition against the Mafia. This is why Santino also said in his speech: 'If these windows don't open, Peppino Impastato's actions will have been pointless'.

Yet Umberto Santino had never known Peppino. Despite belonging to similar political organisations, the 20 miles between Cinisi and Palermo meant that the two had never met. Not belonging to Cinisi, it was easier for Santino and others to identify immediately the key problem – Peppino's group in Cinisi was isolated. If more 'windows' didn't open in the town no real progress could be made.

Isolation and Implosion

Peppino's friends were exhausted. On the evening of his disappearance they had started frantically looking for him just ten minutes after the time he was due to attend a meeting with them. At one point four cars were scouring the town and the surrounding countryside. Inevitably, feelings of guilt started to emerge – could they have done more to save him?

One person with a lot on his mind was Giovanni Riccobono. The morning after Peppino's death Riccobono realised that during the very hours it was estimated that Peppino had died, he had driven his car up the lane towards that very small barn, stopping just 100 metres away from where Peppino's mutilated body was found, before turning back. And earlier on that evening Riccobono had rushed to Cinisi from his job in Palermo because his cousin had told him to stay out of town that particular evening: 'because something big was going to happen'. While he told many other people about such a worrying signal, he hadn't told Peppino because they had recently had a bitter political disagreement.

Over time, people would look back at their actions and, inevitably, with hindsight wonder whether they had done the right thing. At the beginning of his biography of his friend Peppino, Salvo Vitale wrote of their time together at Radio Aut: 'I still feel some remorse about those eight months of intense commitment. I went too far, and I made Peppino go further than he had done up to that point. I encouraged his natural aggression, and let his huge knowledge of Cinisi's politicians and *Mafiosi* explode without restraint.'

But it wasn't as if Peppino's friends collapsed overnight. On the same morning as the Proletarian Democracy rally they had distributed another leaflet in Cinisi, explaining that: 'he was killed by the Christian Democrat Mafia, linked to building speculation, gun running and heroin smuggling'. The defiant tone continued: 'We'll never tire of saying it until the police start investigating the Mafia, specifically those *Mafiosi* who have always acted undisturbed in our area'. They explained that Peppino couldn't have been planting a bomb – his hands were undamaged.

Despite this commitment, Peppino's supporters had a mountain to climb. At times like this you turn to your friends, but politically speaking these young revolutionaries didn't have many friends. Opposition to the Mafia has to be total, otherwise it is meaningless. This very clarity and determination meant that other political groupings wanted to keep their distance from the 'extremists' or 'extra-parliamentarians'.

They discovered this on the morning after Peppino's death, when three of them went to the Communist Party branch to agree on a joint statement. In moments of crisis and struggle Peppino had worked together with Communist Party members. And despite all the theoretical arguments about whether the world could be changed through gradual reforms or revolution, there was an understanding between these two groups in practice; they had the same roots, they were all 'comrades'. But as Piero Impastato recounts, they had a brutal awakening:

> First they said they had to wait for the full-time official to come from Palermo, and we started saying: 'Why the fuck have we got to wait for him? Everybody knows who and what Peppino was.' You have to remember that by this time the police version that Peppino had committed suicide had already come out, and they had some doubts, maybe he did commit suicide or he was a terrorist. So we just told them to get fucked and left.

The next day they produced their own leaflet, which talked about '*a young man* named Peppino Impastato', and that almost accepted the police version . . . years had to pass before . . .

The emotional weight of what he is saying prevents him putting it all into words. The sense of betrayal, of not calling Peppino a 'comrade', was too intense. And as regards local Communists: 'After that we never had any respect for them.'

Despite such anger, given the fact that Peppino was now passing into history, his friends needed to make sense of what had happened, to put his life into some kind of historical context. In the impassioned speeches he gave in the coming few weeks Gino Scasso remembers he often harked back to the history of Communist Party activists of decades before: 'I recounted what I had learnt from an old Communist who had been active under fascism in the Messina area: 'One of us got up to speak and the police arrested him, so then another one stood up, and so on.' I was trying to say: 'Peppino is dead, but the struggle goes on'.'

In the days immediately following Peppino's death, his friends' anger was reinforced by what the communist daily, *L'Unità*, said about the case. The first article was quite long, 10 paragraphs, with the Mafia only being mentioned for the first time half way through. The most probable causes of Peppino's death that were given were terrorism or suicide. The same journalist wrote another lengthy article the following day; the only difference was that he said investigators had 'totally ruled out' the notion that the Mafia had wanted to eliminate a 'dangerous adversary', so the only two causes remaining were suicide or some kind of involvement in terrorism. *Avanti!*, the Socialist Party newspaper, was even more categorical. The headline of its first article was: 'Bomber Blown Up'.

There was considerable interest in Peppino's death. Like today, this was a period when there was a degree of hysteria over the 'terrorist threat', which apparently could pop up even in small provincial towns. It quickly became obvious that all newspapers were on the same wavelength – a unified explanation was emerging. The major establishment daily, *Il Corriere Della Sera*, headlined its first article: 'Left-Wing Extremist Blown Up on Railway Tracks by Own Bomb'.

A net was starting to close around Peppino's comrades. A fog of silence and disinformation was starting to smother Cinisi.

Perhaps more important than the national dailies were the Sicilian papers. The first news in print was published by Palermo's evening paper, *L'Ora*, which mentioned all three explanations for his death without emphasising any one in particular. Over the next couple of days it moved towards the idea he had committed suicide, a theory that was rammed home a week after his death by *Il Giornale di Sicilia*. This paper must have illegally obtained from the police some notes written by Peppino, taken away when they searched his aunt's house for evidence. For anyone who did not know him or what he had been doing all his life, it was very difficult not to believe after reading these notes that he wanted to commit suicide:

> I have been thinking about abandoning politics and life for nine months . . . I have fed my feelings to the dogs. With all the strength left in my body I have tried to claw my way back – but I didn't get there . . . I openly admit my failure as a man and as a revolutionary . . . I would like very much to be cremated, and that my ashes be thrown in the town's public toilet.

Shocking as such thoughts are, many people, particularly young people, say and write things like this from time to time, and although they are genuine feelings in the heat of the moment very few actually take any concrete steps toward suicide.

Aware that a smear campaign was in full swing, the following day Giovanni made a statement to the magistrate investigating Peppino's death. After having been shown his brother's handwritten note he pointed out: 'I believe it can be dated at about spring '77, during some political demonstrations, particularly student ones.' In other words, he told investigators that his brother had written that particular note – and many notes and articles by Peppino were unearthed following his death – over a year before he died. In Palermo people were desperately trying to get their version of the truth out. Two days after his death there was a crowded meeting at Palermo University to hear a speech by the leader of Proletarian Democracy. Sympathetic lawyers were writing reports for the family, taking affidavits from witnesses and collecting evidence.

A truly macabre event had also taken place: in the 48 hours after his death Peppino's friends had gone back to the stretch of railway line that the authorities had abandoned in such a hurry. Fighting off the crows that were picking at the many pieces of his body still around the site, they collected as much of his remains as they could, together with a bloodstained stone taken from the small barn near the bomb crater, and handed them over to a university professor, an expert in forensic science. The reason they had done this was that when they had taken this material to the police, it was clear they were not interested in looking at forensic evidence seriously.

The day after Peppino's death, a demonstration had been organised in the capital, and even though the police had not given their permission, it went ahead nevertheless. As demonstrators were waiting to go into another meeting at the Architecture Faculty, police attacked the crowd, arresting four people and injuring a 16-year-old. Although the Communist Party daily criticised some aspects of police behaviour, it made a point of mentioning: 'yesterday the grave news from Cinisi provided the pretext for a mixed grouping of "extra-parliamentarians" to create serious tension in the heart of Palermo.' Not for the first time, the local establishment just wanted to pigeonhole Peppino and people like him as fanatical troublemakers.

The end result was that in both Cinisi or Palermo very few people heard an explanation as to why Peppino had been murdered by the Mafia. In the meantime, another grim ritual was about to take place – elections for Cinisi council. The election rules stated that all votes for the party list would be counted, including crosses next to Peppino's name, and that if Proletarian Democracy received a sufficient number of votes, it would have its own councillor.

Dead Man's Shoes

Initially it wasn't even clear whether Peppino's friends and comrades wanted to continue with the election or withdraw from it.

Gino Scasso puts one side of the argument:

> I was a member of Proletarian Democracy and had already been elected as a councillor in Partinico. Our view was that we had to carry on campaigning, because withdrawing would have been seen as a retreat. I remember arguing that we needed to get a positive political response from the town because of his murder, and go house to house asking people to vote for him. Not everyone agreed.

The opposing view was more 'extremist', in the sense that people felt taking part in elections meant 'joining the system'. This is what Salvo Vitale thought: 'Our thinking was that this was something only Peppino wanted to do. It meant going and playing a role within the institutions, and this was something we were totally against.'

Eventually it was agreed that the party should not withdraw, and on polling day Peppino's mother and aunt broke a centuries-old tradition by leaving their house. As recently bereaved women they should have stayed at home in mourning for a month – Peppino had died just five days earlier.

Salvo Vitale describes what happened when they arrived at the polling station:

> there were two flunkeys who were distributing Christian Democrat leaflets. When they saw Felicia and Fara they came up to them to express their condolences, telling

them they were asking people to vote for Peppino and his party. Felicia looked at them with extreme pride, but almost with disgust, and never said a word. As soon as the two women walked past them they started giving out their leaflets again.

Despite the hypocrisy of the Christian Democrats, 264 people voted for the name 'Peppino Impastato' on the ballot paper. This was 6 per cent of the vote, and technically meant that he was elected. Relatively speaking it was a high vote, far higher than he had scored when he was alive, and not far behind the Communist Party, which received 10 per cent of votes. On the down side, the Christian Democrat vote increased significantly, from 36 per cent to 49 per cent. In all likelihood, the tension created by Peppino's death had led to a concentration of Mafia votes for their traditional allies.

The next issue was: who would be the councillor?

Since Peppino's death odd things had been happening in town. The house where he lived with his aunt Fara had been broken into five times, but nothing was ever stolen. A house in the country owned by Pino Manzella, where Peppino's friends had kept his remains overnight before taking them to Palermo, was broken into and turned upside down, although again nothing was stolen. Another two houses were also burgled.

Nobody knew for sure what was going on, although many people had heard a rumour that Peppino – always so well-informed – had a dossier that potentially contained all manner of secrets. Most of his friends had received several phone calls, but whenever they picked up the receiver the line went dead. All of this seemed coordinated in some way. In a normal society many people would tell the police, who were not difficult to find – the town had been flooded with police and military vehicles worried about the 'terrorist threat'.

But the general view of Peppino's friends that the police were in league with *Mafiosi* increased their sense of vulnerability. And more than anything thing else they were bound to be afraid to some extent – after all, they believed the Mafia had just murdered their friend. They could also see that the press and establishment parties were only talking about terrorism. So no *Mafioso* was questioned and none of their houses were searched.

Felicetta Vitale recalls the change in mood:

> After Peppino's death we had lots of visits from activists who came to pay their respects. But many of them came in through the back door: because Badalamenti's house was so close to ours they didn't want to be seen coming in. Radio Aut got a load of threatening calls along the lines of: 'now we've killed your leader, the rest of you better watch yourselves.'

Peppino's comrades in Cinisi were disoriented; his death suddenly and brutally revealed the reality of their weakness and isolation. In the end it came down to this: was anybody brave enough to step into Peppino's shoes? If they did, their party – and the people who had voted for him – would expect his substitute to continue Peppino's work as a Cinisi councillor.

A crisis meeting was held in a pizzeria on the beachfront that separates Cinisi from Terrasini. Gino Scasso recounts:

> I remember I turned up with a copy of the electoral regulations; I was a councillor and I wanted to give them some advice but I can remember one of them poking fun at me.
>
> The mood that dominated was fear, but I don't want to blame anyone, this was something perfectly natural and normal. But this meant they didn't want to take responsibility for anything and were trying to pass the buck on who would become councillor. Everyone started to find an excuse for not being a councillor. For example, one of the most experienced of them started to say he had a full-time job, and so on.

Over the next few years the role of councillor was rotated between a few of the candidates on the party list, but nobody really had their heart in it. One of the main reasons was their political assessment of what it meant to be a councillor; apart from Peppino, most of the group had always thought it was a waste of time.

So essentially, from now on the battle to defend Peppino's name and ideas would be fought out more in Palermo than in Cinisi. One aspect of this fight would be to avoid him suffering a second death – 'buried' by the justice system, the media and the political establishment as a terrorist or somebody who had committed suicide.

13

The Light Behind the Blinds

When Felicia Bartolotta Impastato went to the Palermo courthouse with her sister Fara and son Giovanni on 17 May 1978 to talk to the magistrate investigating Peppino's death, it was just a week before her 62nd birthday. Peppino had died eight days earlier. She had neither spoken in public, nor talked to journalists or officialdom before. Despite her son's very public activities, in order to protect him she had never talked to anyone outside her family about what she knew about the Mafia. Outside the courthouse a journalist she had never met asked her whether she knew Cesare Manzella and she said she didn't. But the reporter knew Felicia wasn't telling the truth, so he asked her again, reminding her she had gone to his funeral. Then she admitted in a quiet voice, 'he was my cousin'.

Felicia was torn: she still respected her Mafia husband who had died the year before, and who had tried to keep their son alive. Besides, she came from a culture where women were seen and not heard. But she also admired her son's commitment, and finally decided to speak to Sicily's main newspaper:

I've got one goal – to make it clear that my son Peppino didn't commit suicide and that he wasn't a terrorist. I'm certain that my son was killed. The murderers' aim was to make Peppino appear as somebody violent who was going to plant a bomb, in order to discredit him in the eyes of townspeople, public opinion and his fellow political activists.

Felicia had taken her first public step, the first of many. But the reason she went down that road wasn't really because of one good journalist – who tragically would be murdered by the Mafia early the following year – she had been discussing her position intensely with her son and others.

Just as he did at the funeral, Giovanni was pushing for the family to campaign openly for justice. Peppino's younger brother had never really engaged in anti-Mafia activity consistently; but now he began to make up for lost time. Felicia's instinctive response was to keep quiet: 'In the beginning I didn't want to speak out because I was worried they'd kill Giovanni as well.' But Peppino's younger brother was coming out of the shadow his elder sibling had cast, he wasn't going to take no for an answer. Felicia continues: 'we argued all the time, because I used to get scared. So my son brought these lawyers along and they persuaded me – "By not speaking you are harming the memory of your son".' And, just in case she suddenly backslided, he had another card he was prepared to play: 'Giovanni told me he would have started telling everyone I was mad.'

Even the quiet and shy Aunt Fara, who had moved in with her sister Felicia after Peppino's death, eventually started to speak up. A few months after Peppino's death she gave a sworn statement in which she ripped into the two official reasons given for his death. As regards the suicide note the police found, she recollected precisely when it was written – nearly a year before his death, and went on to state:

> I can confirm that towards the end of his life my nephew was calm; he was even happy because his political activity

was going well. I'm aware of a letter he wrote quite a while ago, when he was in disagreement with other members of his party . . . I insist in the most categoric terms possible that my nephew did not intend to commit suicide.

She was equally forthright in her attack on the police's notion that Peppino went out to a secluded piece of railway track in the dead of night to plant a bomb: 'he had never been there, he didn't know that place. They killed him first and then took him to the railway line. It's impossible that my nephew thought about doing something like that, because he fought for workers and ordinary people and could never dream of a criminal act such as blowing up a train.'

Yet the family had a mountain to climb; all the major parties, the media and the police were against them.

In order to understand what happened from then on a basic explanation needs to be made: the Italian legal system is distinctly different to that in most Anglo-Saxon countries. In Italy the police collect evidence, arrest suspects and sometimes question them, but it is judges, also known as investigating magistrates, who have overall responsibility for both investigations and then mounting court cases.

The other key difference is that these individual magistrates rarely come close to the British stereotype of reactionary public schoolboys sitting around in Mayfair clubs drinking brandy. Essentially they are appointed through a kind of civil service selection procedure, therefore you find people from all walks of life in this position. One of the most famous of recent years, Antonio Di Pietro, came from a poor family that emigrated to Germany to work in a car factory. Di Pietro studied hard, and in the early 1990s was perhaps the individual most responsible for bringing down the entire Italian political ruling class in a series of corruption scandals. Because of their commitment to democracy, some magistrates can be popular heroes in Italy. And in Sicily the occupational hazard of investigating the Mafia means they can also become martyrs, such as Giovanni Falcone and Paolo Borsellino, killed in separate car bombings in 1992.

So if the family had any hope in the months after Peppino's death, it lay with the investigating magistrate. And some moves were made; almost immediately after Peppino's death Judge Rocco Chinnici ordered a ballistics investigation into the kind of explosive used at the scene. Then things slowed down, as they do so often in the Italian justice system. A ray of light emerged 18 months after Peppino's death, when Chinnici ordered the seizure of Cinisi council documents, many of them relating to accusations made by Peppino. Another positive development was the obligatory legal notice to Giuseppe 'Hod Carrier' Finazzo – a local builder and Badalamenti henchman – that he was under investigation.

But this investigation wasn't a priority for Chinnici. In July 1983 he issued arrest warrants for Totò Riina and 200 other *Mafiosi*, a major attack on the organisation. He was to pay for this with his life – *ammazzarono* – by the end of the month he was blown up by a car bomb. After his death, Chinnici's private diary was published, shedding light on some of his thinking, which tragically he did not have time to develop into action. At one point he defines Francesco Scozzari, the deputy prosecutor who took part in the examination of the site where Peppino died, as 'a revolting turncoat, servant of the Mafia'.

But the huge bomb blast that killed Chinnici and two others was just one of the consequences of a ferocious Mafia war that had started two years earlier.

The *Mattanza*: The Second Mafia War

For years, Sicilian fishermen used to follow tuna fish to their feeding grounds, and then slowly trap them in their nets. The boats would move together, raising the nets out of the water. Then hundreds of fish would be gored with harpoons, so much so the sea ran red with their blood. This was the *mattanza* – a good as description as any of the Second Mafia War that broke out 23 April 1981.

This date was the birthday of Stefano Bontate, one of Badalamenti's allies on the Commission and a major *Mafioso* in his own right. As he was returning from his birthday party in his new limousine, the Corleonesi delivered their own present – *ammazzarono* – a salvo of bullets that totally disfigured his face and body. The Corleonesi, under Totò Riina, had finally made their move.

Two weeks later Badalamenti's other main ally on the Commission, Salvatore Inzerillo, was also out in his new car. He thought he was safe because he had just taken delivery of a brand new bullet-proof Alfa Romeo. But Riina's men had done their homework. They had done some tests on a jeweller's bullet-proof display case and discovered that heavy fire on a small area would shatter the glass. Their research paid off and Inzerillo was killed.

This was just a taste of what was to come. In the following months 200 men of this losing faction were murdered in the province of Palermo. Over the next two years around one thousand people were killed. Much of this killing was a delayed reaction, certainly as regards Badalamenti's own situation within the Mafia, as he had already been 'retired' as head of the Mafia three years earlier.

In a normal job, when someone is 'retired' from an organisation they tend to get a nice card from workmates and start drawing a pension, but obviously the Mafia isn't like this. How Badalamenti actually lost his dominance of the Commission in 1978 remains shrouded in mystery. Again, this is only to be expected; news is fragmentary because the Mafia hardly post accounts of their discussions on the Internet.

In the long term, what got Badalamenti 'retired' was the drugs trade. His clan was wading through piles and piles of money and had never wanted to share it with the people from the hill town of Corleone, whom they called 'peasants'. So the Corleonesi slowly built up their support among smaller gangs, particularly in Palermo. And, as we have seen, they received large amounts of money from a series of high-profile kidnappings, which they then invested in the drugs trade. But all the while, they were developing their military firepower.

Strategic differences arose over how to deal with the authorities. One controversial area was how to behave with 'friendly policemen', an issue that can only be described as a hornet's nest. The relationship between a corrupt policeman and a top criminal generally works both ways – but invariably the criminal gets the better deal as long as he's allowed to continue his illegal activities. It was known in Mafia circles that Colonel Giuseppe Russo had told local police to give Badalamenti an easy ride in his hometown. The issue was: what would Badalamenti offer in return? The worry wasn't that some small-fry *Mafioso* would be arrested, but that Badalamenti would get rid of a serious rival by fingering him to the police.

Although this was unlikely because it goes against all Mafia instincts, in a growing situation of internal tension people started to think Badalamenti might just try to get rid of his rivals by non-violent means. Crucially, Russo was an efficient crime fighter who had many *Mafiosi* arrested, sometimes apparently by torturing suspects – so his links with Badalamenti made things all the more worrying. This is why in one Commission meeting the proposal was made to kill him. Significantly, Don Tano voted against Russo's murder, thus saving his life. According to Mafia wisdom the killing would cause more trouble than it was worth; there is no way the police would not turn Sicily upside down if the Mafia killed a senior officer. That was Don Tano's argument, but others were wondering why he wanted to keep this dangerous police contact alive.

The issue was finally settled in August 1977, when Russo was gunned down in the main square of Ficuzza, in an attack personally led by Totò Riina. It was another challenge to Badalamenti's authority.

Badalamenti was the leader of the Mafia, but people wouldn't obey him. He even started losing votes at meetings, and the leader of the Mafia up to 2006, Bernardo Provenzano, once took the unheard step of mocking him: 'Uncle Tano, what you're saying isn't right, that isn't how things are at all. It seems like you've banged your head on something.'

The tipping point for Badalamenti's 'retirement' came in spring 1978. The Commission had earlier discussed whether to murder another senior *Mafioso* and had decided not to go ahead. When the man in question (an ally of Riina) was murdered anyway, Riina accused Badalamenti of involvement, thus rendering nonsensical his leadership of the Commission.

Why didn't Badalamenti move against Riina and Provenzano earlier? We don't know for sure, although we know meetings were held in one of his villas in the hills behind Cinisi to discuss a pre-emptive strike, but nothing came of them. At one such meeting, held the very month that Peppino died, his closest associates could see all the danger signals. Some were demanding immediate war on the Corleonesi, others advised caution: 'At the moment we can't act openly in your support. If we do they'll go crazy.' Badalamenti was sitting out on the veranda and was silent; his faction didn't make a move so for him all that beckoned was 'retirement'.

So why didn't he launch an attack, and why over the next three years did Riina and his men not attack him? Again, nobody knows for sure. Much of the speculation is that everybody knew he had powerful political friends – so both he and his enemies felt he was protected and therefore 'untouchable'.

If so, that would explain why all bets were off by 1981. The Corleonesi had had enough of Badalamenti hovering around like a king who had lost his crown. They were also tired of harassment from the police; the 'peasants' had never cultivated friendships within government or the criminal justice system. While Badalamenti always said 'we can't declare war on the state', this is just what the Corleonesi did.

First, though, they had to get rid of Don Tano, who had been replaced on the Commission by his cousin Antonino since 1978. Even before then Antonino would stand in for him at meetings if Tano was in prison. The Corleonesi had been working on Antonino for a while, and after he had hinted many times that he was going to lead them to his cousin they lost patience, killing him in August 1981.

The following month another Cinisi Mafia boss, Procopio Di Maggio, was attacked outside the petrol station he controlled. Like Badalamenti, he had his finger in the pie of the local airport; driving staff and passengers around the airport he had easy access to the baggage hall. In this attack, although he was shot in both the liver and a kidney he managed to drive his attackers off. Two years later he survived another attempt on his life: a group of killers headed towards him as he was chatting in the main square in front of the council with Salvatore Zangara, secretary of the local Socialist Party branch. Di Maggio reacted fast and avoided the bullets while Zangara, who was totally innocent, was killed and three others wounded. 'Shorty' Di Maggio then drew his pistol and unsuccessfully tried to catch his attackers.

In other words, Cinisi was being turned upside down.

Gabriella Ruffino had married a nephew of Don Tano, Silvio Badalamenti, and remembers the period well:

> All the Badalamentis were already in hiding. If Silvio knew where they were they would have kidnapped him, instead they wanted to send a message to those who were hiding the Badalamentis – that they might get killed as well.
>
> 'When did I know we were in danger?' I often went to Cinisi because I've got relatives there, and as I was crossing the Corso this car was coming down, being driven by a very good friend of mine. Every time we meet we have a chat, he asks me how I am, and so on. He was the owner of a bar, and as you know, you can hear everything in a bar. I went up to him, and he had this expression as if he couldn't see me. I raised my hand to say hello but he's got this blank look about him, as if he can't see.
>
> What I saw was him thinking, 'Why did I have to meet her today?' For the first time I saw this bottomless black well in his eyes, and for the first time I was frightened. When Sicilians decide they don't want to say something their

eyes become black wells – their pupils grow enormous and all you see is your own reflection.

He was frightened. My husband wasn't a *Mafioso* – if I'd been the wife of a *Mafioso* he would have said hello to me. But maybe it could have been dangerous for him to show he was my friend. This was the first moment I got wind of something.

Very soon after, Silvio Badalamenti was murdered.

On another occasion, a few days before Christmas 1981, Felicia Impastato woke up in the early hours:

> I found the doors wide open. I went and looked to see whether the police were there, and I saw an officer from Cinisi I knew who said they were searching the house. Finazzo had been killed and his wife said she suspected it was Peppino Impastato's brother. 'What do you want?' I shouted at them. 'Isn't one enough for you? There's nothing here. Go and look for the murderers in the houses of *Mafiosi*.' They found posters against the Mafia and a few dollars brought over by my sister. Me, my son and his wife were sat on the bed while they emptied everything and looked all over.

Giuseppe 'Hod Carrier' Finazzo, construction manager and Badalamenti henchman, had just been murdered. But why raid the Impastatos' house – hadn't they publicly rejected the Mafia tradition of vendetta three years earlier? Whatever else could be said about them, Giovanni and his mother were certainly not involved in the Mafia. Either the police simply wanted to harass the family, or they had a crude Mafia mentality and therefore investigated following typical *Mafioso* logic according to which, despite all evidence to the contrary, the Impastatos sooner or later were bound to react like *Mafiosi* and launch a revenge attack.

The following month, January 1982, Giacomo Impastato was murdered. Son of 'Leadspitter' Impastato, brother of Peppino's father, what had really caused his death was his marriage to Agata Badalamenti, daughter of one of

Gaetano Badalamenti's brothers. Nobody was too young for the Corleonesi – in November 1982 the 17-year-old son of Antonino Badalamenti, Salvatore, was murdered because he had sworn revenge for his father's murder. Across the Atlantic, in New Jersey another two nephews were killed, Matteo and Salvatore Sollena – the latter was found in the boot of a car wrapped up in a rubbish bag, having been shot several times.

In November 1983 Riina's men dressed up as nurses and entered Carini hospital, killing 64-year-old Natale Badalamenti in his bed. But, despite all these deaths the Corleonesi had still not eliminated their main target, Gaetano Badalamenti. Another close relative, Agostino, fled to Germany, but Riina's men found him in February 1984, tortured him, shot him once and then knifed him 12 times. Back in Cinisi, three days later another Impastato, Luigi, was murdered. He was the son of Giacomo, so was Peppino's cousin.

In all, Badalamenti lost 17 relatives. But the wily old fox was long gone from Cinisi even before most of his relatives were killed. Sometime between 1981 and 1982 he had left his hometown for the last time, taking his wife and two sons with him.

All of this *mattanza* produced changes, the smallest of which was in Cinisi. The surviving members of Badalamenti's clan were terrified, all their certainties had melted into air. Felicia noticed a chink of light: 'in town people only stopped criticising my son after their own children had been killed'. But in such a thoroughly Mafia town, most people simply kept their head down and waited to see, once the shooting stopped, who would emerge as top dog.

The biggest changes occurred in Palermo and Rome. With such a massive scale of bloodshed it became increasingly difficult for individuals within the institutions to connive with the Mafia, and compromised politicians found it far more problematic to oppose anti-Mafia legislation. Incredibly, the crime of 'Mafia association' – essentially Mafia membership – only entered the statute books in 1982.

Turning the Corner

Yet the death of just one person, Peppino Impastato, had already produced some changes.

The first-ever national anti-Mafia demonstration was called to commemorate the first anniversary of his death. Around two thousand people marched through Cinisi, along with a massive police presence. The broadcasting of Peppino's *Crazy Wave* monologues from loudspeakers placed up and down the Corso created a powerful effect.

It was a significant success, with people coming from all over the country, and Giovanni was one of the speakers. Felicia remembers: 'For the first time ever there were demonstrations with people stopping outside the house of a *Mafioso* and shouting, "You're a murderer." How my heart used to pound . . . I shouted louder than them.' It was a show of strength and defiance that temporarily turned the tables: 'When demonstrations took place in the early period, Badalamenti left home for two or three days and only came back when things had calmed down.' Events like this were glimpses of the possibility that *Mafiosi* could be exposed and publicly humiliated, creating a completely different climate in town.

A leaflet advertising the event had argued: 'We believe the time has come to end the widespread belief that views the Mafia as a limited phenomenon, a remnant of the past, a subject for novels and blockbusters.' It had been co-produced by Umberto Santino's research centre in Palermo (which was now named after Peppino), and was strongly influenced by his thinking:

> There were two reasons why I decided to name the Centre after him and why we decided to dedicate so much of our lives to keeping his memory alive and to achieving justice: firstly I realised Peppino was a unique case in Sicily – there had never been anyone who got involved in an anti-Mafia struggle who came from a Mafia family. Secondly Peppino, albeit in an under-developed fashion, had a modern way of analysing and fighting the Mafia. In other words he was half way between the battles of decades ago and new

ones. But all of this had nothing to do with any personal 'friendship'. Maybe for Anglo-Saxon readers this destroys the stereotype of Sicilians only getting involved in things if there is some kind of personal friendship involved.

Despite this increase in an understanding of the Mafia, which was broadcast publicly, problems were far from solved. A month after this demonstration it was announced that Giovanni Impastato and Umberto Santino were going to stand for parliament. Two days later, Giovanni explained, 'They attacked my shop at night, shooting it up. They deliberately killed my dog, which was inside.'

It must have been hard for all those campaigning, particularly those living in Cinisi, not to think about some kind of act of revenge – to raise morale if for nothing else. After all, what would it take to make a few petrol bombs and throw them at *Mafiosi* construction lorries or shop fronts in the dead of night? And besides, in a town like Cinisi it was not difficult to get hold of guns.

This frustration would sometimes come out during the early demonstrations to commemorate Peppino's death. Giuseppe Nobile remembers a Proletarian Democracy leader called Emilio Molinari who gave a speech in Cinisi on 9 May 1982, saying: 'The *Mafiosi* who are moving here among us now should pin back their ears and listen very carefully – we don't like getting involved in vendettas, but if any of us were to come to any harm, we'd know what we have to do.'

This was Nobile's response:

> I was a member of the same party, and because we were holding our conference primaries I criticised Molinari's speech by saying: 'It's fundamentally wrong that someone comes in from the outside to such a problematic town as Cinisi and says something so dangerous – and then leaves.' Later Molinari came up to me and explained that in fact it had been the Cinisi comrades who had asked him to say this.
>
> I really couldn't understand where all this was coming from – after all, Proletarian Democracy got just 1.5 per

cent of the vote, and there was a huge downturn in social and trade union struggles. And I'll go further: after that speech everyone left and went home, and the only people left were me, Gino Scasso and Giovanni Impastato. Given that there was an election on, us three went round the town at night putting up posters. After a speech like that they could have cut all three of us into tiny little pieces, no problem.

His fear was perfectly justified; all *Mafiosi* were extremely jumpy at that time, it was right in the middle of the Second Mafia War. But luckily nothing happened to them, and nobody was ever foolish enough to start acting like a *Mafioso* and launch even a symbolic act of revenge.

For many years these campaigners would suffer defeats and setbacks. Andrea Bartolotta, who had known Peppino since the first year of secondary school, remembers: 'it felt like we were shipwrecked on an island of indifference, virtually condemned to irrelevance and isolation, almost as if we had the plague.' But after a while they began to be compensated by small token victories. The first real step forward occurred in May 1984, six years after Peppino's death, with a court reaching a verdict that he had been murdered by the Mafia because he campaigned against them. So he had not killed himself during an act of terrorism. But the verdict also stated that it was impossible to identify his murderers.

The institutions had slowly come round to the viewpoint of the family and their small group of dedicated campaigners. In the very month he died, Felicia and Giovanni had outlined in a sworn statement to police that in his last speech Peppino made it clear that if elected (something everyone expected) he would have brought more scandals out into the open. As they pointed out, this 'behaviour is very different to that of somebody unbalanced or frustrated'. And they continued: 'People who want to commit suicide are demoralised, without any apparent future, not people who plan their schedule and organise a series of commitments for the following days.'

All told, the lights were beginning to burn brighter behind the blinds of the Impastato household on the Corso. Since the death of her son, Felicia Impastato had virtually never left her house: 'Apart from a few people, I don't want to look into the face of anybody from Cinisi.' One of the few people she did see was the actor Gaspare Cucinella: 'I went to visit her sometimes, but it broke my heart to see her, to listen to her talk.'

Felicia didn't even go out to attend her younger son's wedding to Felicetta Vitale a few months after Peppino's death, even though she had asked Giovanni to get married. Apart from friends of the bride and groom, a scandal half-emerged many years later that another group of people had taken a very close interest in this marriage, and it wasn't the Mafia. Secret service agents took down the number plates of all the cars that attended the service, and Giovanni was subject to surveillance for approximately two years. The reason? The same deranged but desperate desire to try to link Peppino's family and friends to terrorism.

Felicetta was now the daughter-in-law of Peppino's mother, and fully supported her decision to cut herself off from nearly everyone else in town: 'After Peppino's death she hardly ever went out. One of the times she felt obliged to go out was when friends or relatives were ill, or had had an operation. But she never even went shopping. I would buy her everything she needed. And she never wanted to stop mourning: she always wore black.'

Despite her self-imposed isolation, Felicia understood that small changes were occurring, changes that made her more relaxed about Giovanni's activism. Speaking in 1984, at the end of the Second Mafia War, she said:

> Now that some of them are dead or have disappeared, who knows where they've ended up? I'm a bit calmer. I used to hear him come in late at night when I was in bed and I used to say: 'Why didn't you come home earlier, son?' Now when he leaves I'm happy, I think to myself: 'at least he's away from here'.

Meanwhile Don Tano's star continued to wane. After disappearing from Cinisi he had flitted between central Italy, Spain and Brazil, all the while importing huge amounts of heroin into the United States. He was finally picked up in Madrid in 1984 as part of an international investigation. More telling than his capture was his conviction: at the end of the mammoth 'Pizza Connection' trial held in New York, in June 1987 he was given a 45-year sentence for drug trafficking.

Six months later hopes rose once more when it was announced that Peppino's case was to be re-opened. The most successful anti-Mafia magistrate, Giovanni Falcone, went to speak to Badalamenti in his US jail, but as ever Don Tano was saying nothing. So, not for the first time, in March 1990 the case was again closed. For Falcone it was a difficult time too: despite having convicted 342 *Mafiosi* in the 1987 'maxi-trial', he was often isolated within the Palermo courthouse. Not only did he escape an assassination attempt in June 1989, he was passed over for promotion and was frequently attacked in the press through a series of anonymous letters, probably written by one of his fellow magistrates.

In July 1990 campaigners suffered one of their most demoralising setbacks, which fittingly came from one of the most tainted leaders of the Christian Democrats, the Neapolitan Antonio Gava. Ignoring the 1984 court verdict, as minister of the interior he announced that because Peppino had not been killed by the Mafia, his family was therefore not entitled to compensation as Mafia victims. It wasn't that the family wanted to get rich, they had always said they would use the money to educate people to break free from the Mafia. What made such a decision so outrageous was that Gava was commonly held to be close to the Neapolitan Mafia, the Camorra.

A further setback was to follow in February 1992. Probably influenced by the scale of Riina's violence, another court verdict stated that it was unlikely that Badalamenti was involved in Peppino's murder – it was much more likely to have been the Corleonesi. In any event, the case was closed again because no new evidence had been found.

But in the very same month a sequence of events began at the other end of Italy that would unleash a tidal wave of political change, destroying Christian Democrat dominance, and with it, the cosy relationship the Mafia had enjoyed with them.

The Floodgates Open

One day in February 1992 a virtually unknown magistrate, Antonio Di Pietro, organised the arrest for bribery of an equally unknown Socialist Party hospital manager in Milan. Mario Chiesa was caught red-handed taking a bribe worth £4,000 from the businessman who hoped to win the cleaning contract for his hospice. When the police burst into his office, Chiesa was trying to flush the equivalent of £9,000 down the toilet from his previous appointment. After his arrest he admitted to demanding bribes for every contract he awarded, from cleaning to meat supplies. The poor meat supplier had started with giving Chiesa the occasional gift, then in the early 1980s the bribes grew to silver plateware and works of art, and then Chiesa began demanding works by specific artists. The people who died in the hospice were then farmed out by Chiesa to another Socialist colleague, who in turn demanded a rake-off from funeral parlours for the right to bury them. The price per dead body was about £50.

Chiesa quickly implicated other Socialist politicians in Milan, such as Bettino Craxi, prime minister for much of the 1980s. From Milan investigations spread to Rome, and quickly the Christian Democrats were found to be up to their necks as well. Over the next two years – day after day, week after week, month after month – scandal after scandal emerged, and party after party disintegrated due to mass arrests or a collapse in their votes.

The party that had been at the heart of Italian government since 1945 was collapsing, and this produced huge instability in Sicily; the Mafia no longer had a reliable political structure from which they could demand protection in exchange for votes. Not for the first time, Riina and the Corleonesi decided to attack the state head-on, just to remind people in power that they still had to reckon with the Mafia. But this was at a time when the Christian Democrats no longer had support from their electorate – support for the political system was at an all-time low.

The anti-Mafia judge Giovanni Falcone was the first to be killed, in May 1992. A massive bomb exploded underneath the motorway between the airport and Palermo, just as his car was passing, killing him, his wife, and three members of his police escort. Six weeks later his long-time partner, the second most successful anti-Mafia magistrate – Paolo Borsellino – also died in a car bomb. Both these funerals became mass events where the people of Palermo, and some police officers, vented their anger on a political class that had allowed the Mafia to grow so powerful. On one memorable occasion, mourners inside Palermo Cathedral, many of them police officers whose colleagues had died as part of these magistrates' armed escort, jostled the head of state and the chief of police, while outside the crowd chanted, referring to these individuals, 'Mafia out of the cathedral'.

The 'Palermo spring' had begun. Leoluca Orlando, an anti-Mafia politician, became mayor of Palermo with an unprecedented majority in 1993. Far more important than that was the fact that public opposition to the Mafia grew, street committees were formed, and many did not disappear after the first emotional outbursts. In essence, a new generation of anti-Mafia activists had emerged. Sicily had changed, forever.

Back in her house in Cinisi, Felicia Impastato, although she could not speak standard Italian and did not go out and get involved in these events, also understood things were different: 'Something changed after the death of Borsellino and Falcone . . . people started to understand and think, "So when they killed Peppino, it was for the same reason!" . . . He might have been just a nipper, them lot was judges and grown-ups. Only then did they understand that in Cinisi you needed loads of Peppinos.'

In Palermo an unexpected stroke of luck also occurred one day in 1992. As part of their activities at the Peppino Impastato Research Centre Umberto Santino and his wife Anna Puglisi run a press-monitoring service and give their clients a daily round-up of Mafia-related news. One day Puglisi noticed an article that mentioned a new Mafia supergrass named Salvatore Palazzolo, from Cinisi. He was helping magistrates with other cases, but Santino and Puglisi suggested to the Impastato family lawyer that he ask magistrates to interview Palazzolo about the Impastato case, given that he was a member of Badalamenti's gang. In some ways the signs weren't promising, as after a while it transpired that Palazzolo was only cooperating with the authorities because he knew Riina wanted to kill him. In other words, he hadn't decided to make a clean breast of all he knew because he had seen the error of his ways, so he was not cooperating across the board.

Meanwhile, the battle for justice was slowly beginning to gain support in a wider context. In November 1994 Palermo council named a street after Peppino, very near to the main jail. Two further events occurred in May 1995: first the Palermo provincial council passed a motion demanding the reopening of the Impastato case and secondly the Terrasini sea front was named after Peppino – only for the road signs to be ripped down less than a month later. Finally, in May 1996, 18 years after his death, Cinisi council finally named a street after Peppino.

The wheels of the Italian justice system grind outrageously slow. Following further sworn statements and dossiers from Santino's research centre and from the family, Peppino's case was opened again in February 1996. The following month the same people demanded an investigation into the police, accusing them of perverting the course of justice. Things were lumbering forward: a year later Judge Gian Carlo Caselli announced that he was considering bringing Badalamenti to trial as the instigator of Peppino's murder. Some things never changed though; a few days later threatening graffiti appeared in Cinisi and other areas nearby, attacking Judge Caselli.

Finally, nearly twenty years after Peppino's death, it was announced that Gaetano Badalamenti would be brought to trial for ordering his murder, and much of the evidence would in fact be provided by the supergrass Salvatore Palazzolo. Felicia and Giovanni Impastato had a poster put up in Cinisi immediately. While welcoming the news, it also criticised:

> the heading-off of investigations by the police who, instead of helping to find those responsible, did everything they could to destroy Peppino's reputation and make his fellow comrades guilty.
>
> We demand that everything comes out, bringing Badalamenti to trial immediately and dealing with all those who for twenty years have held back the search for truth.

With its big, bold black typeface, it was a real slap in the face for the police officers who had protected the Mafia, and a clear provocation in such a Mafia town. The family had not forgiven or forgotten the often-lonely battle they had been forced to fight.

One of the people keenest to give evidence was Giovanni Riccobono. Back in 1978 he had told magistrates that on the evening of Peppino's death his cousin had told him not to go back to Cinisi: 'because something big was going to happen'. The fact that his cousin knew what was going to happen beforehand clearly implicated him directly or indirectly. This was yet another shock for Cinisi – somebody breaking ranks with the deeply held notion of family solidarity. Riccobono himself recounts what happened next:

> the opinion that many people had of me in town totally changed. This was because after, hearing the magistrate had issued an arrest warrant against my cousin – even within my family people took a really bad view of me, saying I had betrayed my family. More than once my father wanted to kick me out, but my mother and brothers agreed with the stance I had taken.

> The real reason I left town for a few weeks was that when I'd walk past people on the street I'd hear them mumble 'grass'.

When he returned to Cinisi he went to see Peppino's mother, who drew his hand over her heart: 'Giovanni, I've lost a son. If you don't feel up to it, don't go down that road – I'll always love you whatever you do.'

She had the same reaction 20 years later:

> When Felicia heard I was going to testify in Palermo and confirm all that I had said 20 years earlier, when I was at her house she took me into the back room. Then she took me by the hand and said that if I didn't feel up to testifying against Gaetano Badalamenti she wouldn't hold it against me.

But perhaps the person who was most anxious to go to court was Peppino's mother. Felicia finally got her day in court in October 2000, 22 years after the death of her son. Now aged 84, she could hardly walk and sometimes misunderstood what she was being asked. But when she found an outlet for her anger, she was direct and defiant: 'They smashed his skull with rocks then they took him to the railway track putting a bomb around him here, as if he was a terrorist. But it was the *Mafiosi* who were the terrorists.' Her son Giovanni summed up how the tables had been turned in all these years, and showed how his confidence had grown, telling Badalamenti: 'My brother has turned you into a small-town wanker.'

Don Tano was looking and listening on a video link from his jail in the US. As ever, he was as silent as the grave. Felicia looked up at the screen and said: 'that man murdered my son'. Her deposition was an extremely fraught moment: she was a vital witness for the prosecution, so if she gave unreliable testimony it could be a serious blow to the whole case. The defence lawyer did the work he was paid to do, trying to lay traps and get her to contradict herself, showing that she couldn't distinguish between fact and her own imagination. But she got through the test, and the evidence started to pile up against Badalamenti.

Felicia couldn't make the trip to hear the verdict 18 months later, having recently been diagnosed with asthma. Many people did make a special effort to get to the courthouse though; a demonstration called by the Palermo Social Forum against the Berlusconi government decided to stop protesting and go instead to the prison courtroom to hear the verdict. Don Tano had already let it be known he would not listen to the verdict, so the video link with his New Jersey jail was switched off. Badalamenti received his first conviction in an Italian court for 33 years – a life sentence for having organised Peppino's murder.

Giovanni was in court to hear the verdict. Despite his customary good manners, he could not hide his anger about the people who were equally responsible for almost a quarter of a century of torment:

> I feel angry, because getting to the truth after 25 years, when we could have reached it immediately, makes you angry . . . it makes me angry to know that there are men in the institutions who have been accomplices in perverting the course of justice. Our task now is to continue the work done over these years with the Peppino Impastato Research Centre, and to continue searching for the truth about what happened.

The harsh reality behind this long-delayed conviction was devastating for the authorities. It had been obtained for two reasons alone: first it was thanks to long-term campaigning, which was often ignored or discouraged by the authorities; secondly it was due to the testimony of supergrasses. From the moment when Peppino's friends and comrades fought off the crows to collect his remains, the police in particular had ignored what even the leaves of Cinisi knew.

The Hundred Steps

The authorities managed to save some face in late 2000. Nearly two years earlier, parliament's permanent Anti-Mafia Commission had set up a committee to investigate the 'Impastato case'. It heard dozens of witnesses and examined hundreds of documents in its many sittings, and although it presented a stark picture of police incompetence and what was in essence protection of the Mafia, it did not have legally binding powers.

Yet, in a surprising departure from normal parliamentary procedure, out of respect for the family's long years of campaigning, the committee decided to deposit the official copy in the Impastato household. Felicia hugged the three members of the commission who came to deliver it, whispering in their ears in Sicilian: 'Today you have brought Peppino back to life.' All three men, professional politicians for decades, broke down in tears.

In terms of public exposure, this event paled into insignificance compared to something else that had emerged a few weeks earlier, the release of a film on Peppino's life entitled *I cento passi*, (*The Hundred Steps*).

The film was made on quite a low budget. The director was not particularly famous, and most of the cast were Sicilian actors largely unknown to Italian cinema audiences. Named after the distance between the Impastatos' and Don Tano's house on the Corso, *The Hundred Steps* was a huge artistic, commercial and political success. It became the second-largest grossing Italian film of the last 10 years, essentially due to word-of-mouth recommendations.

It won a Golden Lion award at the Venice Film Festival for best screenplay; indeed, such was the interest in the film – shown also throughout the country in schools and at trade union festivals – that even the screenplay quickly sold 100,000 copies in paperback before the DVD became available. The director and crew had received a lot of help from the Impastato family and people who had campaigned for justice for so long. In the final scene of Peppino's funeral many of the extras were people who had been at his real funeral back in 1978. Fittingly, the director gave his award to Peppino's mother.

The film's huge success meant that the annual commemorations in May became much bigger. In 2002 over a thousand people marched from Carini to Cinisi, a distance of ten miles that took over three hours – but once again most doors and windows stayed shut as it passed through town. As the march passed Don Tano's house on the Corso somebody ran out and wrote on it: 'you stupid and ignorant murderer – thank you Peppino'. Three whole days of meetings and cultural events were organised, in an event that was now globalised; many marchers were carrying Palestinian flags. One of the speakers, Haidi Giuliani, whose son Carlo had been killed by the police at a demonstration in Genoa the year before, reminded people that there had been many Peppinos and Carlos.

The following year a different kind of problem arose: the local archbishop 'forgot' about the anniversary march, held every year for the last 25 years, and declared that celebrations of the patron saint of the town would be held on the same day. The authorities now had a problem – would they allow just one march or both? Giovanni said that the commemoration 'will happen anyway, even without authorisation'. The family released a statement saying that *Mafiosi*: 'are not only those who shoot, but also those who want to erase the memory of those who have fought the Mafia until their last breath'. The archbishop's procession was held on another date.

Felicia was now too frail to leave her house, and would greet supporters from her doorstep. Her favourite month of the year was May, as many more people would visit and remember what her son had stood for. In many ways her life's work was over, but people wouldn't stop knocking on her door: from Boy Scouts to politicians, it was literally 'open house' at the Impastatos. By speaking out, Felicia and Giovanni had broken a taboo, by trusting strangers their behaviour was the very opposite of a Mafia family. She once commented on journalists' expectations of meeting her: 'They think beforehand: "She's Sicilian, she won't say very much." On the contrary, I have to defend my son, I have to defend him politically. My son wasn't a terrorist, he fought for very concrete and positive things.'

Entering the house, you would now hear her before you saw her, as she came shuffling out of her bedroom in the back. The tapping on the floor was caused by Felicia moving a kitchen chair in front of her for support: the Impastatos were not rich, there was no point in buying an expensive Zimmer frame when an old wooden chair would do just as well. Her mind and face were far more lively than her body, now bent by age. What characterised her expression more than anything else was her sweet but determined smile, which often verged on a sarcastic smirk when she wanted to stress a point she thought you hadn't understood.

As Cinisi's *Mafiosi* died off one by one, over more than twenty years she often drank to their death. One day at the end of April 2004 Salvo Vitale raced to her house to bring her a bit of news, and to ask her whether she wanted to raise a glass to the death of Badalamenti. Age had not slowed her down, as she told him: 'My son, when I heard that pig had died, I finished the bottle.'

The following day she was as incisive as ever, talking to the press: 'I want to know the names of those who helped him for so many – too many – years. *Mafiosi*, politicians and some policemen were all in on it together. And together they misled investigations into Peppino's murder. Why are judges hesitating about starting new investigations?'

One thing she would often say was that her house was alive and full of people, whereas a hundred steps away Badalamenti's was empty and locked up. Occasionally Badalamenti's widow comes from Castellammare del Golfo to air it, but now it is just inhabited by ghosts.

14

The Bells of St Fara

I n Italy every day of the year bears the name of a saint, and small towns tend to guard the reputation of their local saints jealously. So in many ways it was fitting that the asthma attack that caused Felicia's death two weeks before Christmas 2004 occurred on the day named after Saint Fara, the patron saint of Cinisi.

There is a sarcastic remark used in nearby towns to provoke people from Cinisi – 'What a miracle St Fara has done! The church is closed but the bells are ringing!' The implication is that people from Cinisi often make a lot of noise, but what they're doing and saying is essentially empty and pointless. The response to Felicia's death showed that, on the contrary, her life had had enormous substance.

Given the recent successes of *The Hundred Steps*, the conviction of Badalamenti and the Anti-Mafia Commission's report, Felicia's death became a news item on most television channels. All national newspapers had an article the following day, Cinisi council declared that the day of her funeral be a day of official mourning, that is, an invitation for shops to shut. They also organised a commemoration in the council building, inviting the Impastato family.

The head of state, President Ciampi, even sent the family a message of condolence recognising Felicia's 'tireless commitment in defence of legality and justice against criminal lies'. In Rome, the Anti-Mafia Commission stood and gave a standing ovation in her memory. The family also received messages from the mayor of Rome and three other towns, the leaders of the country's second and fourth largest political parties, television presenters, trade union leaders, religious orders and school groups. Over the next few days several hundred more messages of condolence were to arrive, including some from Britain, France and Spain – mainly from ordinary people.

Felicia's body was carried out of her house on that rainy December morning by some of the men who had been activists with her son 30 years earlier, such as Giovanni Riccobono and Salvo Vitale, and also by a much younger man, Salvo Ruvolo, secretary of the Cinisi branch of the far left party Communist Refoundation.

Waiting outside were politicians such as the former mayor of Palermo Leoluca Orlando, Left Democrat MP Giuseppe Lumia and a Communist Refoundation regional councillor; while trade unions were represented by the regional secretary of the CGIL federation; another prominent individual was Rita Borsellino, sister of the anti-Mafia magistrate murdered in 1992. The road outside was also crowded, as seven investigating magistrates had come – people who have to travel in armour-plated dark blue cars and with an armed escort because many of their investigations are directed against the Mafia.

Luigi Lo Cascio, the actor who played Peppino in *The Hundred Steps* was also there, as was the producer, Fabrizio Mosca. The film's director, Marco Tullio Giordana, had been working on his next film at the other end of Italy, but immediately left the set to fly down for the funeral. He said: 'It's paradoxical, but I think that, having lost Peppino, she acquired hundreds of thousands of other children.' The mayor of Cinisi was there, as were photographers, journalists, young Communists and other political activists. There was also a group of Boy Scouts from northern Italy who had visited and interviewed her the day before her death.

The funeral oration was given by Umberto Santino, who described what Felicia's house had become in her final years: 'All forms of resistance – be they against fascism, the Mafia or neo-liberalism – met here in the most natural way possible . . . The best of Italy and Sicily has passed through these doors.'

Yet at most there were just 150 people waiting to greet her coffin, and most of them had come from outside Cinisi. The funeral cortege wound its way down the Corso, but the people of Cinisi stayed at home, withdrawing further indoors whenever photographers moved close to their windows. As mourners passed bars and shops, not even the shutters were pulled down as a mark of respect.

It seemed like a bad dream, and very similar to Peppino's funeral; it wasn't as if local people ignored or never took part in funerals.

In September 2000 the son of Mafia boss Procopio Di Maggio disappeared and his dead body was washed up on a beach a few days later. Between five and eight hundred people came to his funeral, while many bystanders applauded and others threw orchids as the cortege passed. All the shops pulled down their blinds on that occasion. In December 2001 Vito Palazzolo died, aged 84. He had been convicted in March of that year, in a trial parallel to Badalamenti's, of having organised Peppino's murder. The local police chief banned a public funeral, 'for reasons of public order' – in other words the authorities would have been too embarrassed to see the level of support he had. Ultimately, nearly everyone ends up identifying with some kind of network that they feel can protect and help them.

One of the reasons local people ignored Felicia's funeral, though, was mere indifference, the desire for a quiet life. Giovanni and Felicetta's daughter Luisa, aged 19, even noticed it among young people: 'When my grandmother died, I heard from a friend my age that she had been told by her mother to stay home, and I thought, in this day and age, that's very sad.' The point Luisa is at pains to stress is that people's indifference influences a given situation: 'I don't think people didn't come because of Mafia pressure. But indifference can also strengthen the Mafia's power.'

Some people, however, stayed away for far 'stronger' reasons. As Luisa's mother, Felicetta Vitale, explains:

> My mother-in-law's funeral caused me a lot of bitterness. It was one of those moments when I thought: 'What are we doing here in Cinisi? Why are we living here? We're always wanting Cinisi to change but it never does.' I wanted to say to people: 'a funeral isn't a political protest with red flags' – but people here can't seem to make that distinction. A funeral is a moment of solidarity, of respect. But even people who have business dealings with us every day didn't come.
>
> I had the feeling that because the Mafia is going through a transition at the moment, people are isolating us again. Some people in Cinisi are compromised with the Mafia, they have too many connections – a good number of local people are in that situation. And showing solidarity with us means showing you're not with them, that's how I explain what happened. Whoever accepts a favour from these people can never break free of them.

Salvatore Maltese knows the town like the back of his hand. A Cinisaro born and bred, he was also a fascist councillor for over twenty years:

> You need to realise that in a town of 10,500 people such as Cinisi, if you put together relatives, people who share the same house, your friends, workmates, employees – there are at least 3,500 people who in one way or another have to live alongside Mafia bosses. This could be because you're a blood relative, or because of marriage, or business links, or because you're employed by them – it's clear then that a *Mafioso* will ask you to hide a gun, or drugs, or to hide them when they're on the run.

This attitude was mirrored at the first council meeting held a few days after Felicia's death. The first item on the agenda was a commemoration of Peppino's mother, but councillors from Forza Italia- the party led by the then Prime Minister Silvio Berlusconi - did not attend, only coming into the meeting afterwards without offering any explanation. Furthermore, the kind of employees the council hires, although in its defence it could argue they are simply a mirror of local attitudes, is revealed by the fact that only three out of a hundred council employees have ever taken part in activities that commemorated Peppino.

Although the family and their friends had achieved justice, and Peppino's story had become known throughout Italy and to some extent abroad, it was clear that the battle he fought was still far from being won. But, as Felicetta Vitale explains, perhaps things have moved forward since Peppino's day:

> People know we are right. But sometimes we say to ourselves: 'why are we bothering here?' Despite the difficulties and discouragement, we've found that our cultural activities work. When we give talks in schools we often see that we've planted a seed that has started to grow. You've got to start from below, from schoolchildren.
>
> Initially it was very difficult to get into schools, the first time we managed to do it was in 1992. In the first class we asked them to make a drawing of Peppino, and in the second and third to write an essay about him. Of course, what happens in school gets back to every family, and as soon as they got back home they were asked: 'what did you do?' The fact that we talked about Peppino, who he was and what he did, really shook people up because so many had wanted to forget about him.
>
> Soon afterwards we got threatening phone calls, mainly from women: 'why don't you mind your own business?', 'why are you upsetting and shocking our kids?', 'who's paying you to do this?', 'why don't you go and get a proper job?', 'why don't you get the hell out of Cinisi?' - and loads of swearwords.

Depressing as that may be, it is a sign that the ideas Peppino stood for still challenge the traditional attitude of general indifference or the showing of respect towards Mafia families.

What has perhaps changed for ever is the open visibility of *Mafiosi* and Mafia behaviour. As Felicetta's daughter Luisa points out: 'Now, to some extent, Sicilian consciousness has moved forward. This is why the Mafia has decided to hide itself away, also because it's dealing in business and drugs so much – all things that can't be very visible.'

Having said that, things have continued to be difficult for Giovanni and Felicetta. Due to the success of *The Hundred Steps*, in February 2001 Giovanni was invited to appear on Italy's premier talk show, *The Costanzo Show*. He attacked some of the opinions Badalamenti's defence lawyers were using in his trial – they had dusted down the idea that Peppino was a terrorist, and also called him a 'good-for-nothing' and a 'layabout'. Giovanni defined such opinions as 'stupidities', and those who put them as 'imbeciles in bad faith'. But although he never named anybody, Badalamenti's lawyer won a case against Giovanni for libel. He was fined £3,500 and the lawyer then moved very quickly, rapidly obtaining a possession order on the family's pizzeria, thus forcing immediate payment. Giovanni commented bitterly: 'not only do they kill my brother, not only do they damage his reputation for over twenty years and blacken his name, but now I get convicted as well . . .' However, the name Impastato was now known nationally, and an appeal fund launched by Umberto Santino's Peppino Impastato Research Centre ended up collecting nearly £30,000.

Sadly, the Impastatos' problems have been more than just financial. Three weeks after Badalamenti was convicted and given a life sentence in 2002, in Cinisi two 'Peppino Impastato' street signs were covered over with signs reading 'Gaetano Badalamenti Street'. And in late November Giovanni remembers: 'They even daubed red paint on the white walls of our shop, in the form of rivulets of blood flowing from a bullet wound.' Felicetta adds: 'I can tell you they looked very realistic.' In June 2007 the attacks resumed: twice in two days acid was thrown at the front door of the familiy house on the Corso, as well as againt the plaque that commemorates Peppino.

Every town has its problems – and Cinisi has more than most – but these difficulties always exist in a much wider context.

The Bigger Picture

The major media story of the week that Felicia died was not her death, but an important trial verdict handed down in Milan involving a man named Marcello Dell'Utri. Such was its importance that as the court retired to consider its verdict the speaker of the houses of parliament phoned the accused to express his 'deep esteem and friendship', while the then Prime Minister Silvio Berlusconi commented 'I would put both my hands in the fire for Dell'Utri'.

Who is Dell'Utri? What distinguishes him more than anything else is his close relationship to Berlusconi. The two first met in 1961, when Dell'Utri left his hometown of Palermo to go to university in Milan. Three years later the 23-year-old Dell'Utri started working as a secretary for Berlusconi's building company. After several years back in Sicily, he moved back to Milan in March 1974 to become Berlusconi's private secretary, a position he held for three years. By 1983 Berlusconi had become a powerful television broadcaster and called Dell'Utri back as number three in his Fininvest holding company. He got involved in politics for the first time at the age of 55, when in 1996 he was elected as an MP for Berlusconi's Forza Italia party. In June 1999 he was elected as an MEP and joined the EU's justice commission; and, finally, became a senator in 2001.

In other words Dell'Utri has been Berlusconi's right hand man for forty years, and one of his most revealing early moves, four months after returning to Milan in 1973, was to employ a man named Vittorio Mangano as a 'stable boy' in Berlusconi's 147-room villa just outside Milan.

So who was Mangano? He was a man who was first arrested by the Palermo Flying Squad in 1965 and charged with illegal earnings; his first major conviction came in

1968 for writing bad cheques, followed by another in 1971 for fraud. During his employment under Berlusconi he served time for fraud, was convicted for conspiracy to receive stolen goods, was arrested and jailed for carrying a knife and once again convicted for fraud and writing bad cheques. Over the next fifteen years he was periodically in close contact with Dell'Utri, and in the meantime was in and out of jail, collecting convictions for drug trafficking, and in 1998 a life sentence for murder and Mafia membership.

At the same time Dell'Utri was faithfully serving his boss and close friend Silvio Berlusconi, including during his two periods as prime minister, but he too had problems with the law. In 1996 it was announced that Dell'Utri was under investigation for Mafia membership, and very soon after he was elected as an MP in Berlusconi's party – thus acquiring parliamentary immunity – although immediately after his election he was found guilty of tax fraud and false accounting. In May 2004 he was convicted of attempting to extort money from a Republican Party senator in a case dating back to 1992. Then in December 2004, the same week as Felicia Impastato's death, he was given a nine-year sentence for collusion with the Mafia, with judges defining him as having been: 'Cosa Nostra's ambassador in Milan for thirty years'.

What is Berlusconi? He was prime minister from 2001 to 2006, and a very controversial one at that. Through tax reductions and further liberalisation of television advertising, his personal wealth doubled in just the first two years of his political leadership of Italy. While he was 'only' the 48th richest person in the world in 2001, by 2005 he had risen in rank to 25th.

But it would seem that he is also more than being a fantastically wealthy businessman and successful politician. The month after he was elected prime minister in 2001 the Court of Appeal of Caltanissetta handed down a verdict against 39 Mafia bosses. Part of the sentence mentioned a 'fruitful relationship, at least economically' between the Mafia and Berlusconi's financial empire. One element in this relationship consisted of 'gifts' made to the Mafia over many years, in the form of 'large sums of money' that were initially cashed by Vittorio Mangano – Berlusconi's 'stable boy'.

The broader issue at stake here is not the behaviour of one individual such as Berlusconi, but that professional politicians and the media are happy to work with and show respect towards people with this kind of track record. While people such as Dell'Utri have a legal right to pursue their activities, the Italian establishment and media legitimises these suspect individuals by giving them air time and treating them the same as untainted politicians.

If we look back at similar figures in Peppino's time we can see that over and over again it is the system that is at fault, not just a few bad apples – let's just look at one man, Giulio Andreotti.

Who is Giulio Andreotti? He was the embodiment of the Christian Democrat Party, holding ministerial office almost without interruption between 1945 and 1992, including seven terms as prime minister.

In late 2002 judges in Perugia handed down a 24-year sentence against a man convicted – together with the Mafia – of organising the murder of a journalist. Obviously this was a hefty sentence for a very serious crime, involving an organisation that has profoundly weakened Italian democracy for decades. Yet Prime Minister Berlusconi immediately defined the sentence as 'justice gone mad', and said it was necessary 'to rebuild true legality'. The Forza Italia spokesperson on justice, Giuseppe Gargani, defined the sentence in the following terms: 'hordes of executioners who insist on eliminating by judicial means an entire political class elected democratically'. In democracies, politicians generally accept the verdict of courts, particularly for serious crimes, yet what is doubly strange here is that the man convicted – Giulio Andreotti (subsequently acquitted on appeal) – comes from a different political party to Berlusconi.

What is equally disturbing is that while Andreotti was waiting to appeal against his murder conviction he was allowed to sit in the Senate and pass laws, and was treated reverentially on the many political talk shows to which he was invited. There was nothing but continuity here: up until 1992 investigating magistrates had asked parliament to lift Andreotti's immunity from prosecution 26 times – and each time they were denied – while all the time his party continued to put him forward as minister or prime minister.

Apart from murder, Andreotti has also been tried for Mafia membership, and in the first verdict of this trial he was convicted of holding a meeting with Gaetano Badalamenti in his office in Rome. In 2003 the Court of Appeal in Palermo decided that had never happened, and that Andreotti had no case to answer for Mafia association up to spring 1980. But he was neither cleared nor acquitted of association with the Mafia; what had happened was that the 'statute of limitations' – the fixed period within which one can be convicted for a crime – had been exceeded and therefore the crime was no longer punishable.

Nevertheless, the court held that Andreotti had lied 23 times and found him guilty of: 'cultivating personal and friendly relations with Cosa Nostra leaders', and meeting with Stefano Bontate, a top *Mafioso* and ally of Badalamenti, murdered in the Second Mafia War. Overall, the verdict referred to: 'Andreotti's generic proximity to the Cosa Nostra faction led by Bontate and Badalamenti' in the very period that Peppino Impastato was murdered.

The establishment's response to this trial was to turn reality on its head: they congratulated Andreotti as if he had been comprehensively acquitted. Berlusconi said he was 'very happy for Andreotti', while the man who was to become prime minister three years later, Romano Prodi, called it 'wonderful news'. The Vatican too expressed 'great satisfaction' as Andreotti was congratulated on a live interview shown simultaneously on several channels.

Despite Andreotti's conviction, Marcello Dell'Utri (despite his conviction) proposed Andreotti as the Italian head of state, the president of the Republic, when the post fell vacant in May 2006, a proposal that was supported by Silvio Berlusconi and many other politicians. Although

Andreotti's bid was unsuccessful, to this day he still passes legislation through the Senate and on television chat shows is treated as one of Italy's most prestigious politicians of all time. His reputation is so good that he recently fronted a major publicity campaign for a mobile phone company.

The only journalists who try to talk to him about his conviction are not highly paid, and do not have an easy time for actually daring to show a critical attitude towards him. For example on 20 June 2006 an amateur journalist named Piero Ricca decided to tackle Andreotti about his criminal record at the end of a public meeting at Milan University. Although Andreotti briefly engaged with the journalist, after a few minutes bodyguards pulled Ricca away. He was then followed outside by police officers, cautioned, taken to a police station, and questioned for two hours.

The Road Ahead

In Cinisi the old Mafia boss Procopio Di Maggio is still alive – he even survived a leap from the third floor of a US hospital when he heard some unwelcome visitors were coming to see him. Nowadays he moves about with two walking-sticks, and most days you can find him hanging around outside the bar at the top of the Corso, watching who goes in or out of the council building.

But the world in which Di Maggio grew up in, the one recounted in *The Godfather* films, is long gone. On Cinisi's Corso you no longer see poor peasants on donkeys. As in nearly all corners of the world, globalisation has arrived here – one of the most visible features are North African and Sri Lankan migrants selling carpets or other trinkets. You won't find straw on the pavement either, but Alitalia in-flight tissues discarded by the many people who work at Palermo's international airport, the area's largest employer.

And given that the world has changed, so too has the Mafia.

Just as the Mafia shifted from dominating a world of agriculture and illiteracy to one of industry and public sector development, it is now adjusting to the recent growth in service industries, privatisation and globalisation. There isn't respectable society and the Mafia, there is a growing 'middle class Mafia', prepared to invest and make money working alongside people who have had professional criminal careers.

So, while drug trafficking, murder and extortion are still part of the Mafia's staple diet, the big growth area is white-collar crime. And apart from the embezzlement of EU and other public sector funds, insurance fraud and identity theft, a major new field of money making is privatised health care.

When Totò Riina was arrested in January 1993 the police found a note in his jacket pocket that mentioned a Sicilian builder named Michele Aiello. Over the next few years Aiello started investing his profits from building by buying up laboratories that process test results. As the Italian public health system started collapsing, he bought a hotel and turned it into a private cancer clinic – which politicians subsidised by arranging a continuous stream of public sector patients. Aiello's clinic (until his arrest for Mafia association in November 2003) quickly invested in extremely expensive equipment, making it one of the top five centres for cancer treatment in Europe, offering treatment which is virtually unavailable in the public health system. Looked at cynically, even a patient who needs kidney dialysis for thirty years is a significant and long-term source of profit.

In other words, dirty money can be recycled by investing in a privatised health system, and a guaranteed stream of business is supplied by corrupt politicians. While Lombardy in the north of Italy, with double the population of Sicily, has just 60 private health centres accredited by the public sector, there are now over 1,800 in Sicily.

Given this kind of bonanza, and the sheer economic weight of a privatised health system, it is inevitable that a high number of Sicilian politicians are also doctors and surgeons; indeed, in one recent case a senior surgeon was arrested and accused (due to his past convictions) of being the Mafia boss for an entire area of Palermo. This is why a recent report by Palermo's special police investigative unit can state: 'It is very worrying to discover that for so many professionals – above all doctors – being in contact with Cosa Nostra is such a natural thing.' As Umberto Santino, president of the Peppino Impastato Research Centre, points out, just as today's professionals try to infiltrate the Mafia, how to mobilise ordinary people against the Mafia needs some new thinking: 'If we want to resurrect the great traditions of anti-Mafia struggles then I think we have to concentrate on people's needs, by placing the problem of unemployment, casual labour and so-called development at the centre of our activities.'

Peppino Impastato fought a very unequal battle; with a small group of local followers he led a campaign against the leader of the Mafia. But a lot of what he did still remains valid – most of all his rejection of the notion that the police, government and institutions are fully committed to eradicating the Mafia. His other major contribution, which is still relevant today, was his constant attempt to create mass disputes around people's immediate needs. Umberto Santino again starts from the past and tries to look forward:

> While it's true that nineteenth-century trade unionism is finished – or is becoming increasingly conservative – I've often argued that we need to create a new kind of trade unionism, and develop new kinds of disputes. At the end of the day this battle must be fought on concrete issues and clear objectives. But it's not easy: people's lives today are so fragmented.

Nowadays politicians frequently try to create consensus by promising their electorate 'empowerment' in their daily lives. Many people at work have to grapple with and try to implement meaningless mumbo-jumbo such as 'synergy', 'mission statements', 'benchmark values' and 'best practice'. Yet in the real world, large numbers of young people are alienated by high unemployment and the authorities enacting repressive legislation against what is often not much more than high spirits; while people in work suffer long hours and job insecurity.

As Santino concludes, stopping the Mafia means concentrating on generalised and radical change rather than new buzzwords, laws and prisons: 'If you don't link the fight against the Mafia to a serious battle for development and real democratic change, then the fight against the Mafia will only consist of people making worthy statements.'

Afterword

Last Night in Mafiopoli

The last interview I did for this book was on the outskirts of Cinisi, towards the mountains rather than the sea. It was nearly dark as the car drove down a *trazzera*, a Sicilian country lane, although I could see the lower slopes of Mount Pecoraro looming up out of the gathering darkness.

The two people I was going to meet had detached themselves from active campaigning quite a while back, although they proudly defended the stand they had taken alongside Peppino all those years ago. As ever, it was a very pleasant chat, so much so that one of them – who had never met me before – was breastfeeding much of the time.

Given they were the last of the many people I had interviewed, it wasn't surprising that they didn't tell me very much that was new. But as I was packing away my digital voice recorder and getting ready to say goodbye, one of them said: 'it's still carrying on today, just look at that house down the road.'

'What house?' I asked, expecting to hear a perfectly ordinary tale of somebody building a house illegally and getting retrospective planning permission from the council.

'The one on the corner. It was owned by a nephew of Gaetano Badalamenti until the council confiscated it.'

'And when was that?' After a quick discussion the general consensus was 'ages', and the only one prepared to put a number to the period said 'about 15 years ago'. I asked more questions, often getting conflicting replies from my interviewees. What was clear was that the council had confiscated it from the Badalamentis years before, and that work to repair it had just started again recently.

One of them told me a story about the morning a few years ago when she had gone to the local fountain to get fresh water, because the mains supply is too chlorinated. As a few women were lining up they looked across at the house – which workers had been cleaning out the previous day – and noticed a large object on the front lawn, wrapped inside a big roll of heavy cellophane. It was a large dog, whose throat had been cut. This is a classic Mafia warning to stay away, or risk suffering the same fate.

I tried to find out more: 'What was the council going to use it for?' They didn't know. 'Why had it been confiscated?' They weren't sure, and although this couldn't be the reason for confiscation, one of them seemed to think when it was first built about thirty years ago the whole thing was done illegally.

I was stunned. After the lengthy campaign for justice, the huge popularity of *The Hundred Steps*, two successful trials, the Anti-Mafia Commission report, the arguments over Felicia's death – why had nobody told me about this before? As I said goodbye there were two questions buzzing around my head: *Why does nobody know anything definite about this?* and *Why has nobody campaigned over the long delay in making use of the building?*

As I got a lift back to the centre of town we stopped briefly outside the house. There wasn't much point getting out as it was dark, but I could still make out that it was a sizeable villa – with up to ten rooms.

The following day I talked to a few people about the Badalamenti house. Salvo Ruvolo, secretary of the far left Communist Refoundation Party, had the vague idea that maybe the council would name it after Felicia Impastato, whereas Pino Vitale knew next to nothing. This was all starting to look very odd: after all these two individuals were among the strongest supporters of the Impastatos and the most vocal opponents of the Mafia in Cinisi.

When my friend Giuseppe Nobile arrived in town we decided to go and have a look at the house in daylight. I couldn't exactly remember where it was, but we bumped into Felicetta's brother who took us there. It looked just as big in the sunshine, and in front of it there was a large drinking fountain for cattle.

The structure looked solid but in need of repair; there was a sign nailed up on the first floor detailing which company was going to do the building work, and a pile of sand out the front. You could walk right into the front garden, which is what I did, and then down towards the basement, which I'd noticed was open as well. Giuseppe stood outside on the pavement, at first I thought because he wanted to act as a kind of lookout, but knowing him it was probably because he didn't want to get his shoes dirty.

The basement was a total mess, all kinds of junk and lumps of concrete were strewn everywhere. A toilet and bathroom had been plumbed in, as had a washing machine and dryer. It wasn't clear whether any of the Badalamentis had ever actually lived in the place, but my interviewee of the day before thought they had. One thing intrigued me: two square holes had been cut into the concrete floor, about one foot deep and four feet square. There seemed no purpose for a hole of that size, so what could they mean? My mind started racing: somewhere to hide drugs, or the beginnings of a bunker to hide away when you're on the run from the police? I didn't have time to go upstairs as Giovanni and Felicetta were waiting to say goodbye.

I told them what I'd learnt about the house. Giovanni said he had heard something unofficially from the council – that it would be named after his mother. He was as tense as ever, and almost apologetic that he didn't know more. But there was a tension in the air. Felicetta remained silent and impassive. They both looked tired. It's not surprising: for nearly thirty years not only have they led a battle against the Mafia and the institutions that protected it, they have also raised a family and run a business. Neither of them needs to apologise to anyone, and I certainly wasn't going to start criticising them after all they've been through. We said goodbye, but when I looked at things in a wider context I still couldn't answer these two questions: *Why does nobody know anything definite about this?* and *Why has nobody campaigned over the long delay in making use of the building?*

As dusk fell Giuseppe Nobile and I drove out of Cinisi up to Partinico, where we met with Gino Scasso. Given that Giuseppi and Gino are both from this town and not from Cinisi they knew absolutely nothing about the house, so they couldn't answer these two questions either.

I was so distracted I forgot to buy my ticket before boarding the train for Palermo, and the conductor wanted to fine me. I talked him out of it, and perhaps made a very convincing case for being 'distracted'. As we walked down the platform at Palermo I started talking to him: 'I'm writing a book about Peppino Impastato and the Badalamentis, have you heard about them?' He nodded almost imperceptibly, which only encouraged me to carry on: 'Peppino had a terrible life, what with the Mafia, all the tensions within his family – and maybe he never even went to bed with anyone in his life. But now I've just discovered that the council confiscated a house from the Badalamentis fifteen years ago and has virtually left it untouched.' I put my two questions to him too, but he just held out his hand, impassively: 'Best of luck with your book.'

Now I was back in the city, Cinisi seemed like another world. Nobody can answer my questions; it all seems so strange, above all in a town that is probably the best known in the whole country for both Mafia domination and anti-Mafia campaigning. As I walked out of the station at midnight I remembered the final episode of the 1960s cult television series *The Prisoner*. After living in an oppressive and surreal community as prisoners for an unknown period, three of them make their way back to London. One of the final scenes is a long shot of one former prisoner outside the Houses of Parliament, gesticulating wildly to a policeman, trying to convince him of where he's been and what he's seen.

The following day was my last in Italy in terms of preparing this book, and I decided to make more phone calls. Other people in Cinisi confirmed the basics of what I had discovered. Despite it being 11am on a Saturday I decided to phone the mayor's house, but was told he was out and would be back for lunch; I phoned at 2pm and he still wasn't back; I left a message but he didn't ring back. This is very unusual: in years of experience nobody has ever refused to speak to me when I decide to introduce myself as a *professore* from the University of Canterbury.

I started to think the mayor was avoiding me and my questions. For a while I got worried, and phoned a journalist to tell him the basic outline of what I knew.

Next morning I noticed something interesting in the local papers: the arrest of the mayor of a town near Corleone accused of Mafia membership. Two local builders were arrested too, as well as the town's 'patriarch', who had already been tried for membership of the Mafia and murdering a policeman. Apparently there was a system of recycling dirty money and manipulation of tenders for council contracts.

What was politically interesting about the mayor wasn't so much the stolen pistol that was found in his desk, but that he was a member of the party that has inherited the traditions of the Christian Democrats – the Union of Christian Democracy. The Sicilian leadership was holding a meeting at the time and the regional secretary commented: 'You shouldn't confuse events which involve individuals with the soul of the party, which is against the Mafia'.'

This meeting was being held to confirm the candidacy of Salvatore Cuffaro as president of Sicilian regional government, a position he had won with a massive vote in June 2001. Such huge support made a few cynics wonder whether he had got a little extra help, but they were dismissed until exactly two years later, when it was announced that he was facing charges of associating with the Mafia – the first time that Sicily's most important politician has ever faced such serious accusations.

The basic fact to understand about modern political life in Sicily and Italy is that Cuffaro didn't resign and wait until his name was cleared. Neither did he resign in February 2004, when further charges of aiding and abetting criminal activities within his administration were laid against him. It is this very track record that encouraged his fellow party members to call for his re-election at that meeting in early 2006. Not only that, but in the meantime Cuffaro stood as a senator in the April general election and was easily elected. Number two on the Union of Christian Democracy list was Calogero Mannino, a former Christian Democrat minister who had been convicted two years before of involvement with the Mafia and given a five-and-a-half-year sentence; again his reputation secured his election to the Senate. Despite – or because of – the fact that Cuffaro's election leaflets were found in the hideout of Mafia leader Bernardo Provenzano, captured during the campaign, Salvatore Cuffaro was comfortably re-elected as president of the Sicilian region in 2006. This is why Giovanni Impastato defiantly argued in a front-page newspaper article: 'We Sicilians have to realise that we live in a region where the majority of politicians are in cahoots with the Mafia, starting with President Cuffaro ... We have to solve these problems and break the links between the institutions and the Mafia.'

These stories surrounding Sicily's most popular and powerful politicians were far more important than *my* story of a house in Cinisi that used to belong to the Badalamentis. Yet, wherever you go in Sicily it is hard not to be reminded of the Mafia's power. Near the motorway turnoff for the airport you come round a bend and notice two brown obelisks in front of you, on both sides of the road, about 40 feet high and about 100 yards apart – this is the same size as the crater created in the motorway, caused by the bomb that killed Judge Giovanni Falcone. And as the plane pulled off the runway I looked out of the window and noticed the railway line where Peppino's body had been blown to bits.

*   *   *

A few days later I finally managed to speak with the mayor. He sounded a bit nervous but agreed to send me all the documents the council had about the house. He said it had originally been built illegally, and handed over to the council about four years ago. Given that he had been elected 18 months ago, and that before that the council was run by government-appointed commissioners for a couple of years, he probably felt he was in the clear. The commissioners – appointed because the government had disbanded the council on suspicion of Mafia infiltration – only came to Cinisi once a fortnight.

In the end I received just one document from the council, and it told a slightly different story. The Badalamentis had originally got planning permission for a bungalow, but had made it 200 per cent bigger by building a first floor and attic level illegally. The house had first been impounded in 1985 by a Palermo courthouse, and was definitively confiscated in 1987 by a Supreme Court verdict. I had been wrong to doubt my interviewee: the house had belonged to the authorities – and therefore to the Italian people – for over 15 years.

Following the Supreme Court decision, the property was managed by a kind of government land registry office. They did nothing with it for 10 years – a whole decade. Then in 1997 it was offered to the police, who turned it down because they said they didn't have the money to renovate it.

Another half a decade passed, and then in 2002 things suddenly started speeding up. But I couldn't help thinking: at that point Gaetano Badalamenti and his henchmen had just been convicted, the Anti-Mafia Commission had recently condemned the police's mismanagement of the investigations and *The Hundred Steps* had been a huge success, surely all of this was no coincidence.

Following a request from the council commissioners the house was now finally handed over to Cinisi council. So the current mayor, elected at the end of the commissioners' mandate, was essentially correct – it had 'only' been council property for four years. The original plan was that it would be used as a headquarters for the municipal police, although there would also be an 'office for legality', in other words a structure that promoted a culture of generalised legality. The current plan has slightly changed, and the intention now is to make it both an 'office for legality' and a youth training centre.

At that point I decided to contact the land registry office to ask for an explanation for such a long delay, and any more information that was available. It has a wonderfully slick website, and has the most impressive 'Code of Ethics' imaginable, brimming with phrases about 'transparency' and 'serving the public'. When I rang them up they promised to send me a report, but when they got round to writing they said their Code of Ethics prevented them from releasing any information. I quoted their Code of Ethics back at them, pointing out these were public documents available to the public, but they ignored me for weeks. When I threatened to appeal to their 'Monitoring Committee' they wrote back, saying that if I 'made unjustified negative statements about the conduct of this office, the same body reserves the right to take legal action'.

Questions and Answers

Despite all that I had managed to find out, nobody I knew in Cinisi had given me sufficient answers to my two questions, so here are my own. My explanation is recounted on three levels: Cinisi, Sicily and national.

The old actor Gaspare Cucinella once said to me: 'Peppino isn't dead' and instinctively I knew what he meant. Nearly thirty years after his death Peppino still casts a long shadow, primarily because it took twenty-five years to establish the truth and obtain justice. His brother Giovanni has got drawn into recounting all of this history, including his brother's activities during the 1970s. As a result of the success of *The Hundred Steps*, if he accepted every invitation he received to go and speak he would spend three days out of four outside Cinisi.

For many years several of Peppino's fellow comrades spent a lot of time campaigning to clear his name, and perhaps felt a bit guilty when they looked back and wondered whether they could have done more to save him. Maybe they were also embarrassed by the fact that soon after Peppino died, large-scale political campaigning in Cinisi perished too. The annual 9 May commemoration is now a national event. The end result has been very positive and significant, as Felicetta says: 'when we started Cinisi was known as the town of Gaetano Badalamenti, now people know it as the town of Peppino Impastato'.

But the prominence of this campaigning over a past miscarriage of justice has meant that people's attention has been distracted from the here and now. What is lacking in Cinisi is a noisy, irreverent and daring opposition against local, national and international politics. Gaspare Cucinella draws a deep sigh before telling me: 'The fight against the Mafia can't just take place once a year. Demonstrations, meetings, films are all fine – but you just can't talk about Peppino – you've got to have "after Peppino" discussions as well. And where is it, this "after Peppino"? It doesn't exist. It's as if Peppino isn't really dead.'

This vacuum is also influenced by Sicilian and national politics. The Mafia is everywhere but cannot be seen. It is murderous but it doesn't kill. The crude domination of a Badalamenti has largely disappeared, as has Riina's strategy of a head-on collision with government. Today, one of the biggest growth areas for the Mafia is privatised health care.

But what has remained constant over the years is the overwhelming evidence of collusion between both Sicilian and national politicians and the Mafia. Politicians are regularly arrested and convicted for links with the Mafia, but at the end of the day the system grinds on. The existing structures of parliament, the police and the judiciary are unchanged. The Mafia finds it relatively easy to do deals with corrupt officials, and so it goes on.

People often find it uncomfortable to look the truth in the face, especially when it is right in front of them. Influential politicians and top business players want to defend their power, wealth and privileges. If that means entering into some kind of alliance with organised crime, then so be it.

While the anti-Mafia industry holds conferences in luxury hotels, passes laws, comments on individual cases of corruption, virtually nobody states the obvious: it is the system that needs changing, not some individuals within it. Dozens of anti-Mafia laws and thousands of arrests since Peppino's time have not solved the problem. As long as we live in a society dominated by the rich and the powerful, these kinds of issues – essentially their strategic decisions concerning with whom they will make alliances – are decisions whose effects on ordinary people will continue to weigh heavily.

Peppino's relevance today is undimmed. Not only did he battle the Mafia but he denounced the dominance of the Church and a rigid family structure, as well as calling for a new classless society. And at the risk of turning a true iconoclast into a saint, I'll end this book with the slogan written on the opening banner carried at his funeral, reproduced in this book: 'With Peppino's courage and ideas we shall continue'.

Bibliography

Although much of the book has been built around interviews, the following books have all been essential: the three volumes edited and published by Umberto Santino's 'Peppino Impastato Research Centre' – *L'assassinio e il depistaggio* (Palermo, 1998), *Cara Felicia* (Palermo, 2005) and *Lunga è la notte* (2nd edition, Palermo, 2003); the parliamentary Anti-Mafia Commission report released in 2000, published commercially as *Peppino Impastato: anatomia di un depistaggio* (Editori Riuniti, Rome, 2001) and finally Salvo Vitale's biography, *Nel cuore dei coralli* (2nd edition, Rubbettino, Soveria Mannelli, 2002).

More general books in English that have been a big help are: John Dickie, *Cosa Nostra* (Hodder and Stoughton, London, 2004); John Follain, *A Dishonoured Society* (Warner Books, London, 1996) and Alexander Stille, *Excellent Cadavers* (Vintage, London, 1995). Three books in Italian that were used frequently are: Alfio Caruso, *Da Cosa Nasce Cosa* (Longanesi, Milan, 2000); Umberto Santino, *Storia del movimento antimafia* (Editori Riuniti, Rome, 2000) and the 1,300-page report of the Anti-Mafia commission published in February 1976, *Relazione sul traffico mafioso di tabacchi e stupefacenti nonché sui rapporti fra mafia e gangsterismo italo americano* (Tipografia del Senato, Rome, 1976).

Other than these, the following sources were used for individual chapters – in some cases they were used in several chapters, but to keep the list short only the first use is cited.

1 Two Deaths

The opening description comes from the April 2002 Palermo Court of Appeal sentence against Gaetano Badalamenti.

2 The Killing Fields

Giuseppe Casarrubea, *Portella della Ginestra. Microstoria di una strage di Stato* (3rd edition, Franco Angeli, Milan, 2002); Giuseppe Casarrubea, *Storia segreta della Sicilia* (Bompiani, Milan, 2005); Giovanni Di Capua, *Il biennio cruciale. L'Italia di Charles Poletti* (Rubbettino, Soveria Mannelli, 2005); Paul Ginsborg, *A History of Contemporary Italy* (Penguin, Harmondsworth, 1990); Franco Grasso (ed.), *Girolamo Li Causi e la sua azione politica per la Sicilia* (Edizioni Libri Siciliani, Palermo, 1966); Pietro Manali (ed.), *Portella della Ginestra 50 anni dopo* (2 volumes, Salvatore Sciascia, Caltanisetta-Rome, 1997); Maria Occhipinti, *Una donna di Ragusa* (Sellerio, Palermo, 1993); Alfredo Pecoraro, *Dai campi e dalle officine. Storie di operai e contadini nella Sicilia dal 1947 al 1970* (Doramarkus, Palermo, 2003); Francesco Petrotta (ed.), *Mafia e banditismo nella Sicilia del dopoguerra* (La Zisa, Palermo, 2002); Giuliana Saladino, *Terra di rapina* (Sellerio, Palermo, 2001); Umberto Santino, *Sicilia 102. Caduti nella lotta contro la mafia e per la democrazia dal 1893 al 1994* (Centro Siciliano di documentazione Giuseppe Impastato, Palermo, 1995) plus several editions of the journal *La Voce della Sicilia*.

3 Hotel Delle Palme

Shana Alexander, *The Pizza Connection* (Weidenfeld & Nicolson, New York, 1988); Danilo Dolci, *The Man Who Plays Alone* (MacGibbon and Kee, London, 1968); Michele

Pantaleone, *The Mafia and Politics* (Chatto & Windus, London, 1966); Umberto Santino and Giovanni La Fiura, *L'impresa mafiosa* (Franco Angeli, Milan, 1991); Claire Sterling, *The Mafia. The Long Reach of the International Sicilian Mafia* (Grafton, London, 1991); Nicola Tranfaglia, *Mafia, politica e affari 1943–2000* (Laterza, Bari-Rome, 2001); Leone Zingales, *La Mafia negli anni '60 in Sicilia* (Terzo Millennio, Caltanissetta, 2003) and *I boss della Mafia* (Editori Riuniti, Rome, 1971).

4 The Man Who Made Leaves Move

Gabriella Badalamenti, *Come l'oleandro* (Sellerio, Palermo, 2002); Mario Francese, *Una vita in cronaca* (Gelka, Palermo, 2000) and Salvo Vitale, 'Gli assassini', *Antimafia*, March 2002.

5 It's in the Air that You Breathe

Vito Mangiapani, *Cinisi. Memorie e documenti* (Grifo, Palermo, 2001 [first published 1910]) and Leonardo Pandolfo, *Cinisi. L'erba della memoria* (Ila Palma, Palermo, 1997).

6 The Impastatos

Felicia Bartolotta Impastato, *La mafia in casa mia* (2nd edition, La Luna, Palermo, 1987); Gabriella Ebano, *Felicia e le sue sorelle* (Ediesse, Rome, 2005); Valeria Pizzini Gambetta, 'Becoming Visible: Did the Emancipation of Women Reach the Sicilian Mafia?', in A. Cento Bull and A. Giorgio (eds), *Speaking Out and Silencing. Culture, Society and Politics in Italy in the 1970s* (Legenda/MHRA, London, 2006); Frederic Sondern Jr, *Brotherhood of Evil: The Mafia* (Victor Gollancz, London, 1959) and several issues of *L'Idea Socialista*.

7 Welcome to Mafiopoli

Pino Arlacchi, *Gli uomini del disonore. La mafia siciliana nella vita del grande pentito Antonino Calderone* (Mondadori, Milan, 1992); Raimondo Catanzaro, *Men of Respect. A Social History of the Sicilian Mafia* (The Free Press/Macmillan, New York, 1992); Alessandra Dino, 'Ritorno a Mafiopoli', *Meridiana*, no. 40, 2001; Saverio Lodato, *Potenti. Sicilia, anni Novanta* (Garzanti, Milan, 1992); Nicola Tranfaglia (ed.), *Cirillo, Ligato e Lima* (Laterza, Bari-Rome, 1994) plus the March 2001 Palermo Court of Appeal sentence against Vito Palazzolo.

8 Bulldozers, Builders and Brothers

Robert Alajmo, *Notizia del disastro*, (Garzanti, Milan, 2000).

10 Crazy Waves

Pino Manzella and Salvo Vitale, as interviewed in the video produced by Antonio Bellia, *Peppino Impastato: Storia di un siciliano libero* (Il Manifesto, Rome, 1998); Anna Puglisi, *Donne, Mafia e Antimafia* (DG Editore, Trapani, 2005) and Radio Aut, 'Radiografia di Mafiopoli', in *Accumulazione e cultura mafiose* (Cento Fiori, Palermo, 1979).

12 And the Windows Stayed Shut

Luca Tescaroli, *Le faide mafiose nei misteri della Sicilia* (Rubbettino, Soveria Mannelli, 2003).

14 The Bells of St Fara

Gianni Barbacetto, Peter Gomez and Marco Travaglio, *Mani pulite. La vera storia* (Editori Riuniti, Rome, 2002); Francesco Forgione, *Amici come prima* (Editori Riuniti, Rome, 2004); Peter Gomez and Marco Travaglio (eds), *L'amico degli amici* (BUR, Milan, 2005); Saverio Lodato and Marco Travaglio, *Intoccabili* (BUR, Milan, 2005); Stefano Maria Bianchi and

Alberto Nerazzini, *La mafia è bianca* (BUR, Milan, 2005) and Livio Pepino, *Andreotti, la mafia, i processi* (EGA Editore, Turin, 2005).

For further information, the main websites are: centroimpastato.it and peppinoimpastato.com. The basic starting point, however, is to get hold of the second biggest grossing Italian film of the last decade: *I cento passi/The Hundred Steps* (2000, Italy, dir. Marco Tullio Giordana); it can be found at sites such as at: internetbookshop.it.

This is neither an academic book that pretends it can detach itself from the world that surrounds it, nor a crime thriller obsessed with describing bloodshed and psychopaths. It is a book committed to ridding the world of the Mafia. This is why a large amount of the profits created will go to the 'Peppino Impastato Research Centre', an organisation independent of the institutions, which for nearly 30 years has survived thanks to both personal commitment and public donations.

Acknowledgements

As the Italians say, this book is *corale* – there is a virtual chorus of voices within it, primarily of people who have conducted a long battle against the Mafia and the institutional collusion it benefits from.

So thanks to all those who agreed to be interviewed: Gabriella Ruffino Badalamenti, Gaspare Cucinella, Pino Di Stefano, Margherita Galati, Graziella Iacopelli, Felicetta Vitale Impastato, Felicia Bartolotta Impastato, Giovanni Impastato, Luisa Impastato, Piero Impastato, Nino La Fata, Salvatore Maltese, Nino Mannino, Pino Manzella, Giuseppe Nobile, Ludovico Pizzo, Giovanni Riccobono, Umberto Santino, Gino Scasso, Pino Vitale, Salvo Vitale and somebody who wanted to remain anonymous.

Equally, I have had valuable help, advice and hospitality – often in ways that were not imagined or planned – from: Giuseppe Di Lello, Mariantonietta Mangiapane, the current mayor of Cinisi Salvatore Palazzolo, Giancarla Pantaleo, Caterina Pellingra, Salvo Ruvolo, Antonella Venezia, Mariangela Venuti and Felicetta Vitale's family.

Two people whose advice and generosity have been invaluable are Giovanni Impastato and Giuseppe Nobile. Of equal if not greater importance has been Barbara Rampoldi's help on earlier drafts.

Thanks also to Paolo Chirco for allowing reproduction of his photo of Peppino. Every effort has been made to trace copyright holders for the images, and the author will be happy to acknowledge them in any future editions.

Index